Illustrators:

Howard Chaney

Ken Tunell

Editor:

Stephanie Avera

Editorial Project Manager:

Karen J. Goldfluss, M.S. Ed.

Editor in Chief:

Sharon Coan, M.S. Ed.

Cover Artists:

Sue Fullam

José Tapia

Art Direction:

Elayne Roberts

Art Direction:

Denise Bauer

Product Manager:

Phil Garcia

Imaging:

Ralph Olmedo, Jr.

Publishers:

Rachelle Cracchiolo, M.S. Ed.

Mary Dupuy Smith, M.S. Ed.

FOCUS ON PRESIDENTS

Author:

Cynthia Holzschuher

Teacher Created Materials, Inc.

P.O. Box 1040

Huntington Beach, CA 92647

©1997 Teacher Created Materials, Inc.

Made in U.S.A.

ISBN-1-55734-497-3

UNIVERSAL EDUCATIONAL ME
CC 008
1005 NORTH ABBE R
ELYRIA. OH 4403

Table of Contents

Using the Pages

How you choose to use the pages in this book depends on a number of factors which may include school district curriculum guidelines, learning levels of your students, your teaching style and goals, or the importance of a particular president to your current classroom theme. The following descriptions of the book's features are intended to help you get the most from each page.

Sections

Focus on Presidents is divided into four sections:

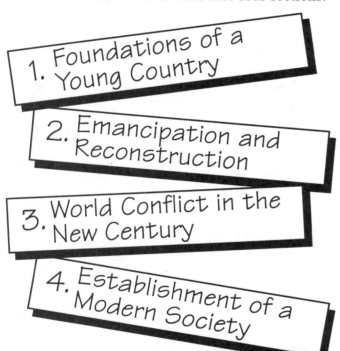

1. Foundations of a Young Country

2. Emancipation and Reconstruction

3. World Conflict in the New Century

4. Establishment of a Modern Society

Choose presidents from the historical period that you are studying. Note that you can use the charts on pages 8, 56, 86, and 110 for quick information about the dates, political parties, states, and important achievements of presidents during each period.

Biographies

The biograpies provided can be read aloud to students, copied for group or individual use, or used for reference.

If you are doing an entire unit on the presidents, copy and distribute pictures as they are studied. Direct the students to glue the pictures to pieces of paper, add important facts, and store them in a designated folder. By the end of the unit, students will have a personal book of presidents.

You may wish to post a large map of the United States on a bulletin board and add a name label for each president, showing the state of his birth.

Use the form on page 4 for help in writing reports about the lives of individual presidents.

Themes

Be sure to include information about the appropriate president in the study of any historical period. These pages will complement units on Famous Americans, Politics, War and Peace, The Great Depression, Government, and the social studies curriculum.

Extensions

At the end of each section there are suggestions for extending the study of the period. Choose those which best suit your classroom needs and adapt them to your students' abilities and learning styles. They are appropriate for whole-class, small-group, or individual use. Check your school or public library for related reading selections.

Student Pages

The student pages cover a variety of skills and learning levels. Assign the pages that are appropriate for your students and feel free to alter the directions, if necessary.

Report Web

Use this web as an outline for your report writing.

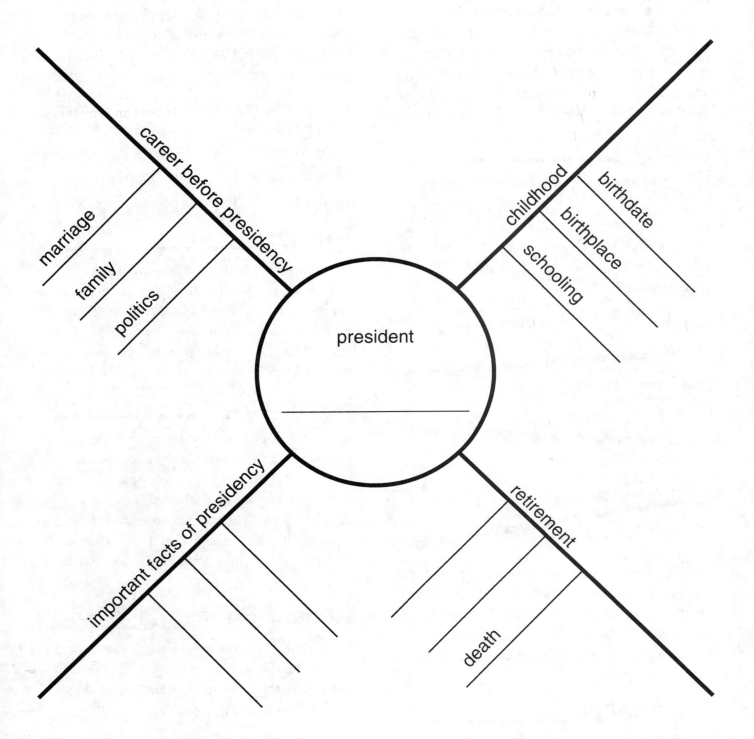

career before presidency

marriage

family

politics

childhood

birthdate

birthplace

schooling

president

important facts of presidency

retirement

death

The Job of President

The Constitution requires that the president be a natural born citizen of the United States and not less than 35 years old. The person must have been a resident of the United States for fourteen years at the time of inauguration.

The president is elected to a four-year term and may serve only two consecutive terms. A president who commits a serious crime may be impeached (removed from office) by a two-thirds vote by the House of Representatives.

The duties of the president are many and varied. He is commander in chief of the army, navy, and air force in times of war and peace. As such, he may direct the movement of forces on land and sea that may provoke foreign countries and cause a war.

As head of state, the president meets and entertains all visiting foreign dignitaries. This may involve negotiating peace treaties, discussing foreign trade policy, appointing ambassadors, or hosting state dinners. The president has the power to sign or veto bills and laws presented by Congress. Once a year, the president delivers the State of the Union address to tell Congress (and the people) how the nation is doing. He presides over his cabinet, a group of professionals appointed to advise him in making decisions.

Ceremonial duties include awarding medals to heroes, laying a wreath on the Tomb of the Unknown Soldier, lighting the White House Christmas tree, and greeting visitors.

Answer the following questions on a separate piece of paper:

1. What are the three Constitutional requirements for the president?

2. How long is the president's term in office?

3. How may a president be removed from office?

4. What are the duties of the president in each of these categories?

    commander in chief　　　　　　head of state　　　　　　ceremonial

Extensions:

- Do you believe it is possible for a minority (female, African American, etc.) to ever be elected president? Why? Why not?
- Would you want to be president? What would you hope to achieve?
- How should you prepare?
- Learn more about political parties. Write for information:
    Young Democrats Club of America, 403 S. Capitol Street, Washington, D.C. 20003 and/or
    Young Republicans National Federation, 301 1st Street S.E., Washington, D.C. 20003.

- What are the best/worst duties of the president? Explain.
- Imagine you are the president's secretary and write a schedule showing the president's activities for a typical day. Include times and locations.
- Make a list of questions you would ask the president if you were attending a news conference this afternoon.
- Choose an article from the newspaper and respond to it as you believe the president would.

Section 1

Foundations of a Young Country

After the battles of Lexington and Concord, it became apparent that the colonists would have a difficult fight for freedom. The American forces camped near Boston, waiting for the British to make a move. The two sides met first at the Battle of Bunker Hill. The British troops had to regroup three times before taking the hill. They suffered heavy casualties. With that battle the British became convinced that the Americans were a serious opponent.

John Adams asked the Second Continental Congress to set up a great American Army led by George Washington. The men were poorly trained and lacked supplies. They had no navy, and worst of all, some colonists did not support the war.

The colonists split into two groups: the Patriots who wanted independence from Great Britain and the Loyalists who opposed the war out of loyalty to Great Britain. In 1776, the Second Continental Congress set up a committee headed by Thomas Jefferson to write a formal statement of independence. He explained to the world why the colonists had to separate from Great Britain. On July 4, 1776, the members of the Continental Congress adopted the declaration.

A year later, British general John Burgoyne believed he could win the war if he captured New York's Hudson River Valley. He intended to cut off the colonists from their supplies, but he miscalculated the distance on the map. The Americans were waiting for Burgoyne and his troops when they reached Saratoga. Burgoyne was forced to surrender.

Washington's army spent a difficult winter at Valley Forge. More than 2,000 men died without adequate food and clothing. By spring the remaining soldiers were renewed with supplies and training from a German officer, Freidrich von Steuben. The Continental Army met with defeat and victory, but they kept alive the fight for freedom.

Washington planned to surprise Cornwallis at Yorktown. The British army was surrounded, and the last battle of the Revolutionary War was won by the Americans on October 19, 1781.

Foundations of a Young Country (cont.)

After the war, America entered a period of rapid growth. The country had won its independence and was free to trade with any country in the world. The foreign money helped to build the new nation.

Cotton became the cash crop of the South. Machines were invented to separate raw cotton from seeds and spin it into cloth. Slavery grew because plantation owners needed laborers.

Some Americans went west in search of new, unsettled lands and opportunity. The pioneers built log cabins and planted gardens. They soon established many small towns, and by 1800, over 700,000 white settlers lived west of the Appalachian Mountains. In 1803, the Louisiana Purchase doubled the territory of the United States. It included all land west of the Mississippi River to the Rocky Mountains and stretched from the Gulf of Mexico to Canada.

A system of internal roads and canals was developed to encourage transportation and link the East and West. The National Road and Erie Canal allowed goods to be moved cheaply throughout the country. Soon, other canals and roadways were opened. In 1827, the first railroad in the country was built to link Baltimore, Maryland, and the Ohio River.

As settlers continued west, relations with Native Americans became more and more difficult. White men disregarded the treaties that granted them land. In 1830, President Andrew Jackson signed the Indian Removal Act. The act said that all Native Americans must move to Oklahoma. This made Indian land available to Southern plantation owners for cotton.

The discovery of gold began a movement west to California in 1848. People were willing to endure hardships in the new territory in the hope for easy money. Immigrants from China joined Mexicans, Native Americans, and slaves working in the mines. America's land now stretched from the Atlantic to the Pacific Oceans. It was a young country with tremendous resources and potential.

Foundations of a Young Country (cont.)

Name/Dates	Political Party	State	Achievements/Events
George Washington 1732–1799	Federalist	Virginia	commander in chief, president of Constitutional Convention, planned Washington, D.C.
John Adams 1735–1826	Federalist	Massachusetts	the XYZ Affair, first to live in White House, foreign diplomat
Thomas Jefferson 1743–1826	Democrat-Republican	Virginia	wrote the Declaration of Independence, Louisiana Purchase, inventor
James Madison 1751–1836	Democrat-Republican	Virginia	British burned Washington, War of 1812
James Monroe 1758–1831	Democrat-Republican	Virginia	Monroe Doctrine, Missouri Compromise, Era of Good Feelings
John Quincy Adams 1767–1848	Independent	Massachusetts	Erie Canal, foreign minister
Andrew Jackson 1767–1845	Democrat	Carolinas	Trail of Tears, spoils system
Martin Van Buren 1782–1862	Democrat	New York	"Bank Wars," Panic of 1837
William Henry Harrison 1773–1841	Whig	Virginia	War of 1812
John Tyler 1790–1862	Whig	Virginia	supported Southern secession, annexed Texas
James K. Polk 1795–1849	Democrat	North Carolina	Oregon Treaty, California Gold Rush
Zachary Taylor 1784–1850	Whig	Virginia	Mexican War hero
Millard Fillmore 1800–1874	Whig	New York	Compromise of 1850, Fugitive Slave Law
Franklin Pierce 1804–1869	Democrat	New Hampshire	three sons died, Gadsden Purchase
James Buchanan 1791–1868	Democrat	Pennsylvania	never married, foreign minister

8

George Washington

Presidential Term (1789–1797)

1st

George Washington, the "Father of Our Country," was born February 22, 1732, in Westmoreland County, Virginia. His father died when George was eleven and his half brother, Lawrence, took over his care. He did not attend school regularly, but by age eleven he acquired basic reading, writing, and mathematics skills. Math was his best subject. He did not attend university. When he was 16, George moved to Lawrence's estate, Mount Vernon, and learned to be a surveyor. He inherited Mount Vernon on Lawrence's death, where he lived for the remainder of his life.

At 26, he married a young widow, Martha Custis, and adopted her two children. They joined him at Mount Vernon. Washington had no children of his own.

George received his first military appointment as a major in the militia during the French and Indian War (1754). In 1758 Washington was elected to the House of Burgesses and expressed his opposition to Britain's unfair taxes and land laws. He was active in resisting British rule. When the Revolutionary War began (1775) the Continental Congress asked George Washington to be the commander in chief of the Continental army.

With a force of about 10,000 men, he faced a difficult winter (1777–1778) at Valley Forge, Pennsylvania. They had little food and were poorly clothed. Those who survived until spring were pleased to learn that France had recognized America's independence. With aid from France, the troops were able to trap the main British force at Yorktown (1781). After the war, Washington returned home to Mount Vernon.

George Washington was a member of the Federalist Party, believing in a strong central American government. His popularity caused him to be elected president of the Constitutional Convention in 1787, and in 1789 he became the first president of the United States. He was elected to a second term, with John Adams serving as vice president. He refused to run for a third term as president.

He died on December 14, 1799, of a throat infection brought on by several hours outside in a freezing rain. He is buried in the family tomb at Mount Vernon.

Suggested Activities/Extensions

1. Do research to learn more about the job of a surveyor. Write a report to explain the duties, training, and tools used. Where might you see a surveyor working? If possible, invite a surveyor to visit your class. Compare the job as George Washington did it with that of a modern surveyor.

2. Brainstorm a list of duties George Washington had as the first commander in chief of the Continental army. How was that job made more difficult because of the time period? Consider difficulties in communication and transportation.

3. About two-fifths of the colonists were willing to fight against the British. They were called Patriots. One-fifth remained loyal to Great Britain and would not participate in the war. Write a debate between a Patriot and a Loyalist regarding the war effort. Which side would you have taken? Explain.

4. Have students brainstorm the advantages and disadvantages of fighting a war on one's own soil. Together, create a chart highlighting the students' ideas. Then have students write about this issue. Use the following questions as a guide: What advantages did the colonists have fighting the war against the British? Why was it difficult to conduct a war from a long distance? What are the disadvantages of having a war fought in your homeland?

5. Research a list of Revolutionary War battles, their locations, who participated, and which side was victorious. Make a chart to show the information.

Related Reading

The American Revolution by Philip Clark, Marshall Cavendish, 1988.

George and Martha Washington at Home in New York by Beatrice Siegel, Macmillan, 1989.

Geroge Washington, Father of Freedom by Stewart Graff, Garrard, 1964.

George Washington, 1st President of the United States by Lucille Falkof, Garrett, 1989.

George Washington, 1st President of the United States by Zachary Kent, Children's Press, 1986.

10

The Star-Spangled Banner

On June 14, 1777, the Continental Congress decided what the flag would look like. The Congress said, "The flag of the 13 United States be 13 stripes, alternate red and white; the union be the thirteen stars, white in a blue field, representing a new constellation." According to legend, Betsy Ross, a Philadelphia seamstress, made this flag from a design given her by George Washington.

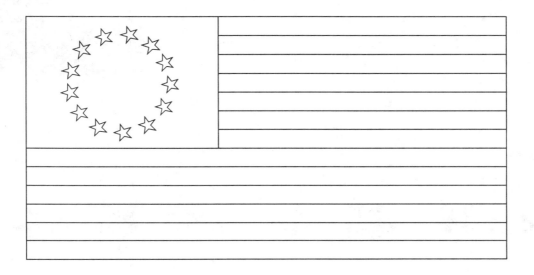

What kind of flag would you have designed? Consider all the events of the time and draw your flag here. Explain your ideas on the back of this paper.

John Adams

Presidential Term (1797–1801)

2nd

John Adams was born in Braintree, Massachusetts, on October 30, 1735. He had two younger brothers, Peter and Elihu. As a child he enjoyed sports, particularly hunting, and school. His father (a farmer and leather craftsman) was concerned that John receive a good education, so in 1751 he entered Harvard College. He became a lawyer and spoke out against British taxation.

He married Abigail Smith in 1764, and they had four children: Abigail, John Quincy (who became the sixth president of the United States), Charles, and Thomas. Their marriage remained strong even during long separations because of Adams' role in the Revolutionary War. In 1775, he led the Second Continental Congress to form the Continental army, and in 1776, he was part of the debates that led to the writing of the Declaration of Independence.

Ill health plagued most of Adams' 90 years. He had frequent colds and chest pains due to Boston's weather, and by the time he was elected president, his hands shook from palsy, and almost all of his teeth had fallen out. In later life, he had cataracts and had to ask his grandchildren to read to him.

Adams was a diplomat in Europe from 1780–1788. When he returned to the United States, he was elected the country's first vice president under George Washington. In 1796, he narrowly defeated Thomas Jefferson for the presidency. The seat of government moved from Philadelphia to Washington, D.C. in 1800, and the Adamses were the first family to live in the unfinished White House.

After his defeat by Thomas Jefferson, John Adams retired to study and write. He lived longer than any other president. Adams died July 4, 1826, from heart failure and pneumonia. He was 90 years old.

Suggested Activities/Extensions

1. John Adams' eldest son grew up to be the sixth president of the United States. How do you think living with a president shaped John Quincy Adams' career choice? Do you know anyone who has followed his father's career? Do you plan to have the same career as your father? Explain.

2. After graduation from Harvard, John Adams became a brilliant lawyer. He often spoke out against unfair British taxation. How do you feel about the tax laws in the United States today? How are you affected by taxes in your daily life? What appropriate ways can people act out against new or increased taxes? Write a letter to John Adams showing your support and detailing some possible solutions to this problem.

3. Adams was a diplomat abroad from 1780–1788. He lived in France, the Netherlands, and Great Britain. Locate the capitals of those countries on a map of the world. Research to find out what a diplomat does. List the responsibilities of United States diplomats today. Share your findings with the class.

Abigail Adams

4. Abigail Adams raised their four children and ran the family farm alone while John Adams was in Congress. She was concerned about independence and equality for women in the United States. At that time women could not attend college or vote. They could not hold political office. Abigail asked that John "consider the ladies" when he was making a new code of laws for the country. Given this information, what general statements can you make about Mrs. Adams? Do you think she was able to influence John Adams' presidential decisions? In your opinion, was she a good First Lady? Explain.

Related Reading

Abigail Adams, "Dear Partner" by Helen Peterson, Garrard, 1967.

John Adams: Second President of the United States by Marlene Targ Brill, Children's Press, 1986.

The John Adamses by Cass Sandak, Maxwell Macmillan, 1992.

The Presidential Palace

James Hoban was an architect who was paid $500 for drawing up the plans for the presidential home. He felt it should be a special house, fine enough for entertaining foreign diplomats but not so elegant as a palace. The drawings were approved by George Washington.

Washington said the oval room would be appropriate for greeting guests and the East Room an excellent place for formal receptions and dances. He felt the house should "grow with the country," so to save money, he omitted the porch and side wings of Hoban's original plans. The cornerstone of the building was laid on October 13, 1792.

John and Abigail Adams moved into the mansion with only six rooms completed. When she arrived, Abigail found the home cold and damp. Servants had to carry water from a half mile away. There was no bathroom. Stone cutters, carpenters, and brick makers were in the house and on the grounds. The gardens were a sea of mud. Abigail found the unfurnished East Room was the best place to hang laundry! On New Year's Day 1801, the Adamses held the first formal reception in an upstairs sitting room. Three months later, Thomas Jefferson was inaugurated president, and he occupied the mansion.

Answer these questions on separate paper:

1. Why was it important that America have a proper presidential house?

2. What were Washington's feelings about the building of the mansion?

3. What was the condition of the home when the Adamses moved in?

Research:

Use an encyclopedia to learn about the changes made to the Executive Mansion over the years. List some of these changes on this chart:

Year	President	Change

14

Thomas Jefferson

Presidential Term (1801–1809)

3rd

Thomas Jefferson was born on April 13, 1743, in Goochand County, Virginia. He had six sisters and one brother. His father was a landowner and public official, representing his county in the House of Burgesses. Young Thomas was sent to boarding school from the ages of 9 to 14. He attended the College of William and Mary and was admitted to the Virginia bar in April of 1767. He practiced law in Virginia and served in the House of Burgesses (1769–1774). Jefferson opposed the British rule in the colonies.

Thomas Jefferson met Martha Skelton in 1770. She was a young widow with an infant son. They were married in 1772 and lived at Monticello, his estate in Virginia. The couple had two daughters, Martha and Mary, who lived to adulthood. It is said that Thomas and Martha enjoyed singing and performing music; he played the violin; she, the harpsichord. They were happily married for ten years until her death in 1782.

He was part of the committee which drafted the Declaration of Independence in 1776. Other famous Americans on that committee were Benjamin Franklin, John Adams, and Robert Sherman. Because he represented Virginia, the most powerful colony at the time, Jefferson was chosen to write the document.

He served as governor of Virginia and vice president under John Adams before being elected president of the United States in 1801. He became the first Republican president.

Jefferson said "the best government is the least government." He believed in the rights of individual states rather than the authority of the federal government. In 1803, the Louisiana Purchase almost doubled the size of the country. He commissioned the Lewis and Clark Expedition (1804–1806). Under Jefferson taxes were cut, and slaves could no longer be brought into the United States.

He is credited with the invention of the swivel chair, lazy Susan, pedometer, and a letter-copying press. After two terms as president, Thomas Jefferson retired to Monticello. He founded the University of Virginia in 1819. He died on July 4, 1826, fifty years after the signing of the Declaration of Independence. He is buried in the family cemetery on the grounds of Monticello.

Suggested Activities/Extensions

1. Study the Declaration of Independence. Why was it important for the Americans to break away from British rule? What risks did Thomas Jefferson (and the others) accept when they signed the Declaration? If you had been a member of the Continental Congress, what would you have added to or changed about the document?

2. Thomas Jefferson invented a swivel chair, adjustable writing table, and a plow moldboard. What characteristics are necessary to become an inventor? How would these characteristics make him a good president?

3. He was also an architect. Thomas Jefferson designed Monticello, his home in Virginia, with many interesting, labor-saving devices. Learn more about Monticello. If possible, talk with an architect about the considerations that are necessary in designing a home.

4. Jefferson was also interested in landscaping and horticulture. Look around your neighborhood (or in magazines) to find a home that is nicely landscaped. Why is the design appealing? Visit a garden store and make a list of plants that grow well in your area. Think about what a landscaper must consider when selecting appropriate plants. Draw a landscape plan for your yard.

5. During Jefferson's presidency, Noah Webster began work on a dictionary of the English language. He realized that English was spoken differently in the United States than in England. In 1806 and 1807 he published small dictionaries. What problems do you think Mr. Webster encountered making the first dictionary? How would you have organized a dictionary? What information is included in dictionaries? How would our lives be different without dictionaries?

6. On May 14, 1804, Jefferson sent Merriwether Lewis and William Clark west to explore the Louisiana Territory. Read more about their journey. Write a journal entry and/or make a map about the experience.

Related Reading

The Lewis and Clark Expedition by Patrick McGrath, Silver Burdett, 1985.

The Story of the Louisiana Purchase by Mary Kay Phelan, Crowell, 1979.

The Story of Monticello by Chuck Mitchell, Children's Press, 1970.

Thomas Jefferson and the American Ideal by Russell Shorts, Barrons, 1987.

Thomas Jefferson: Father of Our Democracy by David Adler, Holiday House, 1987.

The Declaration of Independence

Here is a sentence from the opening to the Declaration of Independence.

"We hold these truths to be self-evident, that all men are created equal, that they are endowed by their Creator with certain unalienable Rights, that among these are Life, Liberty, and the pursuit of Happiness."

Rewrite this sentence in your own words:

Complete these webs with examples of "unalienable Rights."

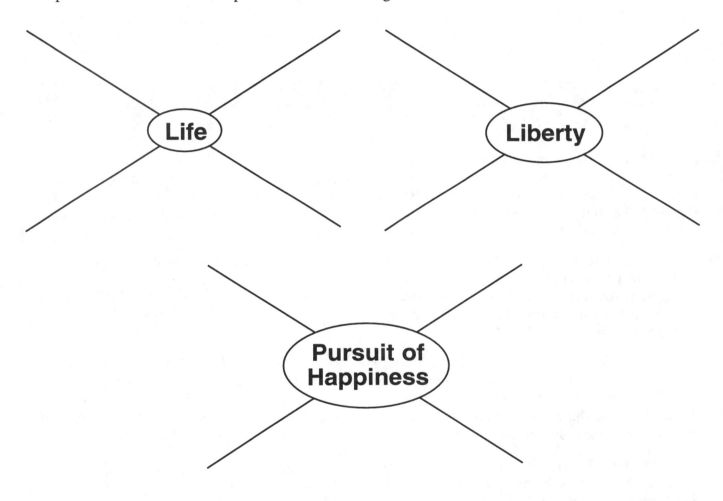

Here are some of the signers of the Declaration of Independence:

- John Hancock
- Benjamin Franklin
- Samuel Adams

- Roger Sherman
- Carter Braxton
- George Wythe

- Benjamin Rush
- Richard Henry Lee

Use an encyclopedia to learn more about one of these men. Write the information on the back of this paper.

James Madison

Presidential Term (1809–1817)

4th

James Madison was born on March 16, 1751, in Port Conway, Virginia. When fully grown he stood about 5' 4" tall and weighed just 100 pounds. Madison grew up on his grandfather's plantation in the Blue Ridge Mountains. Little is known about his childhood. He was educated from ages 11 to 16 by Donald Robertson from whom he learned math, geography, and modern and ancient languages. He said of his teacher, "All I have in my life, I largely owe to that man."

He enrolled in the College of New Jersey (now Princeton University) and graduated in two years. He studied law but never became a practicing attorney. He later served as a member of the Continental Congress (1780–1783) and the Virginia House of Delegates (1784–1786). Madison is called the Father of the Constitution because of his role in the writing of the document. He argued successfully for a strong central government.

Madison married Dolley Todd, a widow with one son, on September 15, 1794. She was a charming First Lady who enjoyed entertaining in a grand style. During the War of 1812, Dolley Madison arranged for the safe removal of national treasures from the Executive Mansion. The Madisons left the White House for three days and returned to a burned-out shell. James Hoban, the original architect of the mansion, took charge of the rebuilding.

On September 13, 1814, British ships were pounding Ft. McHenry in Baltimore, Maryland. Francis Scott Key watched the bombing and wrote the poem "The Star-Spangled Banner." It was later set to music, and Congress officially made "The Star-Spangled Banner" our national anthem in 1931.

The Republican from Virginia was elected to two terms as president. He led the country through the War of 1812 to emerge free of economic dependence on Britain. He favored the gradual abolition of slavery and in 1819 helped found the American Colonization Society, an organization that helped return black slaves to Africa.

Thomas Jefferson paid him this tribute, "I can conscientiously say that I do not know in the world a man of purer integrity . . . nor could I in the whole scope of America or Europe point out an abler head." He died quietly of heart failure June 28, 1836, at his Montpelier estate.

Suggested Activities/Extensions

1. James Madison studied law to broaden his knowledge. He never actually worked as an attorney. How could his understanding of the law help his career in politics? What other careers require a knowledge of law and legal practices?

2. History says that Madison kept lengthy notes on each session of the Constitutional Convention. His account is the most complete existing record of the meetings that produced the Constitution of the United States. Taking notes is a valuable study skill. Try this; work with a partner, read the Constitution, and take notes to summarize important information from each article.

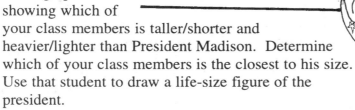

3. James Madison was the shortest and slightest president. He was 5'4" tall and weighed just 100 pounds. Make graphs showing which of your class members is taller/shorter and heavier/lighter than President Madison. Determine which of your class members is the closest to his size. Use that student to draw a life-size figure of the president.

4. Congress debated seventeen days before declaring the War of 1812. A group called the War Hawks were angry because the British had attacked American ships, and sailors and Indians were attacking the settlers in the West. They believed the British in Canada were supplying guns to the Indians. The War Hawks wanted to add Canada to the United States, but Madison felt that the war would be difficult to win. Write a speech that a War Hawk might give in an effort to persuade Congress to declare war.

Related Reading

James Madison by Susan Banfield, Watts, 1986.

James Madison, Fourth President of the United States by Susan Clinton, Children's Press, 1986.

The Madisons by Cass Sandak, Maxwell Macmillan, 1992.

The Father of the Constitution

James Madison was a member of the Constitutional Convention. The delegates agreed that the government should be a republic. In a republic, the people elect representatives to run the country. Delegates to the Constitutional Convention planned a government with three branches: the legislative branch, the executive branch, and the judicial branch.

The **legislative branch** makes the laws of the country. It is made up of the two houses of Congress, the House of Representatives and the Senate.

Activities:

- Do research to learn rules for members of these two groups. What powers does the Congress have?
- What is the vice president's role in the Senate?
- Learn the names, addresses, and phone numbers of your local representatives.

The **executive branch** carries out the laws made by Congress. It is made up of the president, vice president, and the cabinet.

Activities:

- Do research to learn the names and positions of the cabinet members.
- What are the requirements for being elected president/vice president? What powers does the president have?

The **judicial branch** has the power to interpret the Constitution. It is made up of the Supreme Court and all federal courts.

Activities:

- Do research to learn the names of the Supreme Court members.
- Locate recent news articles about decisions made by federal courts.

20

James Monroe

Presidential Term (1817–1825)

5th

James Monroe was born on April 28, 1758, in Westmoreland County, Virginia. He was the second of five children, having one older sister and three younger brothers. His father died when he was 16, and James went to live with his uncle Joseph Monroe. James inherited his father's estate and the responsibility for his younger brothers.

At age 16, he entered the College of William and Mary. After serving in the Revolutionary War, he studied law from 1780–1783 under Thomas Jefferson. He never earned a college degree.

He married Elizabeth Kortright on February 16, 1786. She was often in poor health and had to curtail her activities as First Lady. The couple had two daughters.

Before becoming president, James Monroe was a member of the Continental Congress and the United States Senate. He served his country as Minister to France (1794–1796) and Great Britain (1803–1897).

In 1803, he negotiated the Louisiana Purchase. He was also governor of Virginia as well as secretary of state and secretary of war under James Madison. His long record of public service made him a favorite Republican candidate for the presidency. He was easily elected to two terms.

His presidency, called the Era of Good Feelings, was marked with peace and prosperity for the country. Because of the movement to the West, Monroe encouraged construction of roads and canals. He preserved the balance of free and slave states with the Missouri Compromise which established that states north of latitude lines 36° 30' were to be free and the states to the south of the line, slave. His greatest legacy was the Monroe Doctrine (1823), which became the basis of American foreign policy. In his speech to Congress, Monroe warned the European governments against trying to claim additional territory in the Western Hemisphere.

Monroe stayed in the White House for three weeks after the inauguration of John Quincy Adams because his wife was too ill to travel. Later, they retired to their estate at Oak Hill, Virginia. After the death of his wife, Monroe moved to his daughter's home in New York City. He died of heart failure on July 4, 1831.

Suggested Activities/Extensions

1. Because the British had burned down the White House in the War of 1812, it was not ready for President Monroe to move in after his inauguration. He decided to take a lengthy trip around the country. He began in Washington, D.C., and traveled north to Portland, Maine. From there, he traveled west to Detroit and then turned back southeast to Washington. The trip took 15 weeks. Trace the journey on a map of the United States and list the major cities. Write an itinerary for the president's trip.

2. The economy of the country changed after the War of 1812. Children worked long hours for low wages in the factories of New England. The factory owners provided housing and credit at a factory store. The workers were essentially slaves to the factory owners. Read more about conditions in the factories and write an illustrated summary for a class book about the industrial revolution.

3. President Monroe favored imposing a tax on imported goods in order to raise money for a system of internal improvements. He intended to make European goods more expensive and encourage people to buy products made in America. Do you agree with this idea? Why is it important to buy American products? How do you believe tax money raised from imported goods should be used?

4. In 1817, a group called the American Colonization Society was formed whose purpose it was to end the practice of slavery. They thought the best solution was to return blacks to Africa. They established the colony of Monrovia (named in honor of James Monroe) in western Africa as a new homeland for freed American slaves. Design a poster explaining the position of the Society.

Related Reading

James Monroe: Fifth President of the United States by Christine Fitz-Gerald, Children's Press, 1987.

Kids at Work by Russell Freedman, Clarion, 1994.

The Monroes by Cass Sandak, Maxwell Macmillan, 1993.

"Era of Good Feelings"

This was a brief period in American history when the Republican party had the approval of almost all Americans. In 1820, when Monroe was elected to a second term, he received all but one electoral vote. The Seminole War (1817–1818) had ended, and Florida was acquired from Spain (1819). Five new states, Mississippi, Illinois, Alabama, Maine, and Missouri were admitted to the Union. The Missouri Compromise (1820) established the boundaries for slave and free states, and an interstate system of roads and canals was begun. In his most famous speech, the Monroe Doctrine (1823), the president warned European countries against further colonization in the Western Hemisphere. It was a good time for a very popular president.

Complete this chart with information from the reading. Then, list events for each category that would make the time in which you are living an "era of good feelings."

Era of Good Feelings		
	1817–1825	**Now**
Politics		
Progress		
Peace		
Prosperity		

John Quincy Adams

Presidential Term (1825–1829)

6th

John Quincy Adams was born on July 11, 1767, in Braintree, Massachusetts. He was the eldest son of the second United States president, John Adams. Because of his father's career, he lived in Europe from ages 10 to 17 and learned to speak French fluently. His early schooling was at home (because of the Revolutionary War). He received his first formal schooling at Passy Academy outside Paris. By the time he returned to America to live, he had mastered the Greek, French, Latin, Dutch, and Spanish languages. He attended Harvard University and worked as a lawyer for a brief time in Boston.

When Adams was 30, he married Louisa Catherine Johnson. She was an Englishwoman and the only foreign-born First Lady. They met in London where her father was an American consul. Their marriage was a difficult one. She was unhappy and sickly, suffering from migraine headaches and fainting spells. The couple had three sons.

Before becoming president, John Quincy Adams served as Minister to the Netherlands, Russia, and later, Great Britain. He was a senator from Massachusetts and secretary of state under President James Monroe. He was influential in the writing of the Monroe Doctrine.

John Quincy Adams served only one term as president. Four candidates ran for office in the election of 1824. His opponent, Andrew Jackson of Tennessee, actually received more electoral and popular votes, but because no candidate had won a clear majority, the election was decided in the House of Representatives. According to the Constitution, the House is to elect the president from the top three electoral vote-getters. Henry Clay, the fourth highest candidate, was dropped from consideration. He gave his support to Adams, and on February 9, 1825, the House elected Adams on the first ballot.

Under Adams, Congress approved the extension of the Cumberland Road into Ohio and the building of the Chesapeake and Ohio Canal. The Erie Canal, the first shipping route from the Northeast to the West, was opened in 1825. Adams proposed a high tax on imported goods from Europe to protect the industry in New England. The Tax of Abominations was passed by New England legislators despite organized opposition from the South led by Andrew Jackson.

Adams retired to Quincy, Massachusetts, in June 1829. He eventually became a member of the Whig party and returned to Washington as a member of the House of Representatives. He is the only former president to return to public office. He died on February 23, 1848, two days after suffering a massive stroke at his desk on the House floor. He is buried beside his wife in the family tomb in Quincy, Massachusetts.

Suggested Activities/Extensions

1. John Quincy Adams was the first president to encourage the government's role in making internal improvements. He hoped to create a self-sufficient national economy with the North and South exchanging raw and manufactured goods. Today our country has a well-developed system of roads and interstate highways. Discuss the value of the highway system in your area. Are there any plans for new construction or repairs? What other public works projects (stadiums, nature preserves, etc.) are in your city? How do these internal improvements enhance the quality of your life?

2. Make a chart to show the flow of commodities like fresh food or manufactured goods between different sections of the country. Explain whether most of these goods are transported by truck or rail.

3. On July 4, 1828, the Baltimore and Ohio became the country's first steam powered railroad. Research the history of steam power from the stationary steam engine to applications in water and rail transportation.

4. It is said that John Quincy Adams kept a personal diary every day from ages 29 to 49. He was not yet the president. What kinds of things might he have written? How can we learn more about history from reading diaries that people have left behind? Try keeping a diary for a week (or longer). Later, reread what you have written. What would someone think about you if they read your diary 100 years in the future? What important information could you convey?

Related Reading

Early Travel by Bobbie Kaufman, Crabtree, 1988.

John Quincy Adams: Sixth President of the United States by Zachary Kent, Children's Press, 1987.

Transportation by Robert Gardner, Twenty-First Century Books, 1994.

The Erie Canal

The Erie Canal cut through the Appalachian Mountains and provided the first trade route from the Great Lakes to the Atlantic Ocean. Its 363-mile length was traveled by boats and barges towed by oxen or mules. Because Lake Erie was higher than the Hudson River, there were 83 locks to move boats through changing water levels.

On the map below, label the following: Hudson River, New York State, Pennsylvania, Lake Erie, Buffalo, Albany, Lake Ontario, Rochester, Utica, New Jersey.

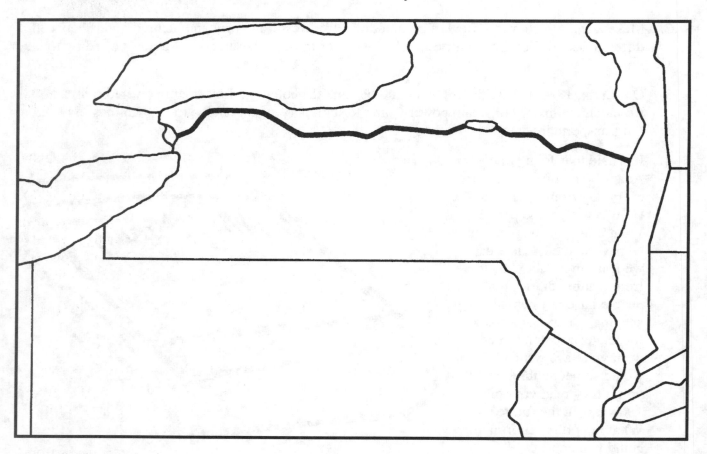

Activities:

1. Write a news article about the opening of the Erie Canal. Include information about who will benefit from the canal, why it is an important event, the date of opening, and the exact route. Add an appropriate headline.

2. Discuss or write your answer for one of these:

   • How did the opening of the canal change trade after 1825?

   • How was the country helped by President Adams' commitment to internal improvements like roads and canals?

   • What kinds of transportation replaced the canals?

   • Imagine life on a canal boat. What would happen on a typical day?

Andrew Jackson

Presidential Term (1829–1837)

7th

Andrew Jackson was born on March 15, 1767, in the Carolinas. He had two older brothers, Hugh and Robert. His father died in a farming accident shortly before Andrew was born. His mother wanted Andrew to become a minister, so from ages 8 to 13 he studied the classics with members of the clergy.

Andrew served as a messenger during the American Revolution. He and his brother Robert were taken prisoner by the British. Jackson is the only president to have been a prisoner of war, having spent about two weeks in captivity. When his mother and two brothers died in the war, Andrew was left alone at age 14. He lived for awhile with his uncles and was apprenticed to a saddlemaker for six months.

He was not a particularly good student and did not want to be a minister, so he went to Salisbury, North Carolina, where he studied law and was admitted to the bar in 1787.

On January 17, 1794, he married Rachael Donelson Robards in Nashville, Tennessee. Because of confusion over her previous divorce, the president and his wife dealt with much controversy during their marriage. The scandal hurt his political career, and Jackson blamed the problems for his wife's poor health and early death, December 28, 1828. The couple had no children of their own. In 1809 they adopted one of Mrs. Jackson's nephews.

Before his election, Andrew Jackson served his country as U.S. Representative and U.S. senator from Tennessee. He easily won two terms and became the first Southern Democratic president. However, his presidency was not without controversy.

In 1830, Congress passed the Indian Removal Act at the suggestion of President Jackson. He believed that the only way to end the fighting between settlers and Indians was to move the Indians to new homes west of the Mississippi River. Jackson tried to persuade the Indians to move voluntarily, but several Cherokee refused. They were rounded up by soldiers and removed by force. About 15,000 Indians made the trip into the new Indian Territory. Four thousand died along the way of cold, sickness, and hunger. The survivors remembered this experience as the Trail of Tears.

Jackson retired to his plantation, The Hermitage, in Nashville, Tennessee. He remained interested in politics until his death from tuberculosis on June 8, 1845. He is buried next to his wife in the Hermitage garden.

Suggested Activities/Extensions

1. Jackson was known as a president of the common man. He was the first president elected from the frontier and the small businessmen, workers, and farmers loved him. A mob of well-wishers followed him into the White House following his inauguration. They became unruly and damaged furniture and the surroundings. It is said that Jackson escaped through a back window and ran to a nearby hotel. Imagine the scene at the White House that day. Draw a picture that shows the gathering of Jackson's "common people."

2. The presidents before Jackson had been refined gentlemen. Choose one of the presidents you have studied. Compare and contrast him with Andrew Jackson on a Venn diagram. Consider their backgrounds, behaviors, educations, opinions, etc.

3. Andrew Jackson was orphaned at the age of 14. What kinds of problems would a fourteen-year old have then and now? What characteristics help a person become successful despite the hardship of being an orphaned 14-year old?

4. The first major national political conventions were held in 1832. Research information about the parties. Make pictures of their symbols and learn what happens at a national convention. Determine the parties of your local politicians.

5. Read more about the Indian Removal Act. The Cherokee tribe had learned to live peacefully with white society, and they asked the Supreme Court for help. Jackson ignored the decision of Chief Justice John Marshall and forced the Indians off their land. Role-play situations between the Court and leaders of the Cherokee. Explore the feelings of all the people (Indians, Jackson, Chief Justice Marshall) involved.

    Within ten years of the passage of the Indian Removal Act, over 70,000 Indians were forced to move across the Mississippi. Since many died on this journey, the trip became known as the Trail of Tears. Have students research the Trail of Tears and subsequent events which forced Indians from their land.

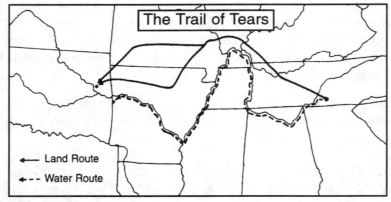

Related Reading

The Alamo by Leonard Fisher, Holiday House, 1987.

Andrew Jackson by Alice Csinski, Children's Press, 1987.

The Life of Andrew Jackson by Robert Remini, Harper, 1988.

Who Let Muddy Boots into the White House? by Robert Quackenbush, Prentice Hall, 1986.

Indian Removal Act of 1830

Andrew Jackson wanted to solve the country's problems. He had spent years fighting on the frontier and knew the problems caused by the Indian wars. He wanted to end the fighting.

Problem: _____

Point of View

Indians	Settlers
_____	_____
_____	_____
_____	_____
_____	_____

President Jackson's Solution _____

_____

_____

Results _____

Bonus

Your Opinion of President Jackson's plan

_____

_____

Your Solution _____

_____

_____

Why is your solution better than President Jackson's?

_____

_____

Martin Van Buren

Presidential Term (1837–1841)

8th

Martin Van Buren was born December 5, 1782, in Kinderhook, New York, to Dutch parents. His father was a farmer and tavern keeper. Martin was the first president born an American citizen, because all the others were born before the Declaration of Independence and were British subjects.

His early education was in a dreary, one-room schoolhouse. At that school he learned the basics and excelled in composition and public speaking. He was apprenticed to study law with Francis Sylvester before the age of 14 and in just one year summed up his first case in front of a jury. After six years with Mr. Sylvester, he became a fine lawyer.

Martin Van Buren married Hannah Hoes on February 21, 1807. She was also of Dutch heritage. The Van Burens had four sons during their 12-year marriage. Mrs. Van Buren died of tuberculosis at age 35, before her husband was elected president. He never remarried.

After a successful law practice, Martin Van Buren served as a New York state senator (1812–1820) and U.S. senator (1821–1828). He was governor of New York for only three months before resigning to become secretary of state under President Andrew Jackson (1829–1833). He resigned that position and later was elected vice president during Jackson's second term (1833–1837). He was the Democratic party candidate for president in 1836 and won the election.

His presidency was marked by a four-year depression called the Panic of 1837. It ruined the American economy. Nine hundred banks in the country failed, and many people were out of work. Despite these problems, the country moved forward with the opening of the first state-supported normal school (for the training of teachers) in Massachusetts and the patenting of the steel plow, mechanical reaper, and telegraph. During the late 1830s, The Underground Railroad, a group of people helping slaves flee the South, was very active.

Van Buren retired to his Lindenwald estate in New York after leaving public life. He enjoyed visiting friends, farming, and fishing. He died July 24, 1862, after suffering an asthma attack and is buried next to his wife in the family plot at Lindenwald.

Suggested Activities/Extensions

1. Do research to learn more about the Trail of Tears, the period during 1838 and 1839 when 15,000 Cherokee were forced to leave Georgia and walk to new government reservations in Oklahoma.

   Write a news article explaining the facts of the situation and the terms of the Indian Removal Act of 1830 (Andrew Jackson).

2. Discuss the effects of patronage in the government. When Van Buren was secretary of state under Andrew Jackson, it became common practice to fire government workers who did not support the president's party. How is patronage practiced today? What jobs change after an election? Do you think it is a good practice?

3. Major changes took place in the banking system during this period. Discuss the purpose of banks, why they must be secure, and the various services they provide. If appropriate, role-play banking practices like filling out withdrawal/savings slips and check writing.

4. If you had been president, what would you have done about the question of Texas? Van Buren felt that it was important to keep the balance between free and slave states. He opposed admitting Texas to the Union. What do you think? Write an essay stating your position. Be sure to support your choice.

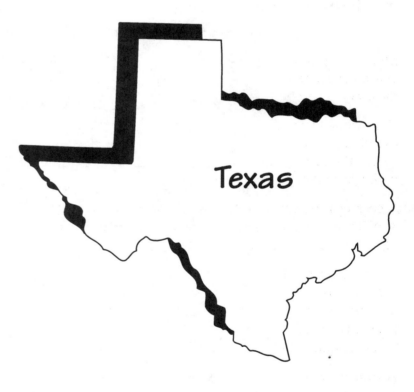

5. Martin Van Buren was of Dutch ancestry. His family spoke Dutch at home. He married Hannah Hoes, who had also been raised in a Dutch home and had a distinct Dutch accent. Take a survey to find which students speak (or know someone who speaks) a language other than English. Make a graph showing students who speak another language at home.

Related Reading

Martin Van Buren by Jim Hargrove, Children's Press, 1988.

Martin Van Buren: 8th President of the United States by Rafaela Ellis, Garrett, 1989.

The Story of Money by Betsy Maestro, Clarion, 1993.

Texans by Gail Stewart, Rourke, 1990.

Panic of 1837

About the time Martin Van Buren was inaugurated president, the people in the large eastern cities of America were experiencing difficult economic problems. Inflation was rising. Food and rent were expensive, and there were few jobs. There was not enough hard currency (gold coins) to go around. Banks began issuing paper money that was of little value since it was not backed by gold. The economy was in crisis.

Some politicians felt that the building of the Erie Canal was part of the reason for the problems. The people who moved west had taken their hard currency with them.

Prior to 1837, Andrew Jackson had criticized the Bank of the United States for being too eager to help wealthy people. He had set up a number of smaller banks to handle government money, but these banks also made unwise investments. Van Buren realized that these banks had been a mistake.

President Van Buren decided the government should withdraw its money from all banks and set up an independent treasury. The new U.S. Treasury would be free of the investment problems that led to the Panic of 1837. His plan was challenged in Congress and not approved until several years later.

Complete these statements, showing cause and effect.

1. Banks printed paper money that was not backed by gold, so_____
   _____.

2. When the Erie Canal was built, people moved west and _____
   _____.

3. Andrew Jackson believed the Bank of the United States helped wealthy people, so _____
   _____
   _____.

4. Because of unwise investments, banks were faced with a shortage of hard currency, so _____
   _____
   _____.

5. Martin Van Buren realized that putting government money in small banks was a mistake, so _____
   _____
   _____.

Bonus: Do research to learn more about our banking system and explain why the Panic of 1837 could not happen today.

William Henry Harrison

Presidential Term (March – April 1841)

9th

Wiliam Henry Harrison was born on February 9, 1773, in Charles City County, Virginia. He grew up during the American Revolution. His early schooling was with tutors on his family's estate in Virginia. He planned to become a doctor and attended Pennsylvania Medical School until his father died and the money ran out for his education. In August 1791, he joined the army.

Harrison married Anna Tuthill Symmes on November 25, 1795. She was the only woman to be the wife of one president and the grandmother of another (see Benjamin Harrison, page 78). Her father was a wealthy Ohio landowner who disapproved of Harrison. Despite this, the two were married in secret. Symmes accepted his son-in-law after he achieved fame on the battlefield. The couple had nine children. Mrs. Harrison never lived in Washington. She was preparing to join her husband at the White House when he died suddenly, one month after his election.

He served the country as governor of Indian Territories from 1800–1812. He negotiated important treaties, opening southern Indiana and Illinois to white settlers. Harrison soon realized the Indians did not always honor the treaties and the settlers were sometimes attacked. On November 7, 1811, Harrison successfully led soldiers against the Indians at Tippecanoe. This battle put an end to the Indian resistance to white settlements in the region. Later, as a major general in the War of 1812, his victory over British and Indian forces at the Battle of the Thames made him a national hero.

Harrison's was the first modern presidential campaign, with songs, rallies, and political advertising. He easily defeated an unpopular President Martin Van Buren. Harrison delivered his inaugural address outside in a cold March wind without a hat, gloves, or coat. Later, he got caught in a hard rain and returned to the White House soaking wet. One month later (April 4, 1841), William Henry Harrison died of pneumonia. His vice president, John Tyler, succeeded him in office.

Suggested Activities/Extensions

1. Learn the symptoms and modern treatment practices for pneumonia. Is pneumonia a fatal illness today? How has medicine changed since Harrison was president?

2. Harrison was the first presidential candidate to make speeches in his own behalf. He did it to prove he was not too old for the job. What do you think he said to convince the people to vote for him? Be a speech writer. Plan (and deliver) a persuasive speech that Harrison might have used.

3. Harrison was made famous by the Battle of Tippecanoe when he invaded Indian country and forced their retreat. After that, he was called "Old Tippecanoe," a name which he used during his presidential campaign. Design buttons and pennants bearing the slogan "Tippecanoe and Tyler, Too."

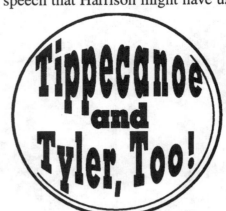

4. Here are vocabulary words related to the Battle of Tippecanoe.

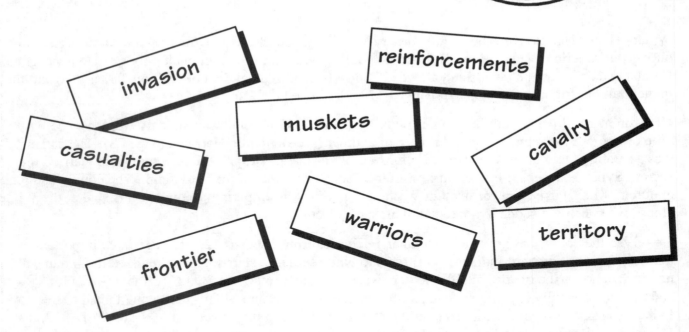

Use these words in a story about the battle or write each word with its definition on an index card. Staple the cards together in alphabetical order to make a minidictionary.

Related Reading

Tecumseh, Shawnee Warrior-Statesman by James McCague, Garrard, 1970.

William Henry Harrison by Christine Maloney Fitz-Gerald, Children's Press, 1988.

One Month as President

William Henry Harrison contracted pneumonia and died one month after his inauguration. He had accomplished very little. Imagine that you were president of the United States for one month. What things would be most important to you? Make a list of what you would like to see accomplished and number them in order of importance.

If you wish, you may work with a group to "elect" a president and designate cabinet members. Determine what each person would hope to do with a month in office.

Education

_____

_____

_____

Welfare

_____

_____

_____

Health Care

_____

_____

_____

Defense

_____

_____

_____

Foreign Policy

_____

_____

_____

John Tyler

Presidential Term (1841–1845)

10th

John Tyler was born March 29, 1790, in Charles City County, Virginia, between Richmond and Williamsburg. His mother died when John was seven, leaving his father to raise eight children. At the age of twelve, the future president enrolled in the preparatory school at William and Mary College. He graduated at age 17 and went on to practice law in Virginia.

On March 29, 1813 (his 23rd birthday), John Tyler married Letitia Christian at her home in New Kent County, Virginia. They were married 29 years and had seven children. Mrs. Tyler did not enjoy the responsibilities of a politician's wife. She lived in Virginia during Tyler's terms in Congress. In 1839, Mrs. Tyler suffered a stroke that left her paralyzed, and she stayed confined to the upstairs living quarters at the White House. She died September 10, 1842.

Two years later, while still president, Tyler married Julia Gardiner in a quiet service in New York City. She was 30 years younger than the president, and their marriage shocked Washington. The president's new wife was younger than his eldest daughter! The new First Lady enjoyed public life and during their final months in office hosted a grand ball at the White House for 3000 guests. The couple had seven children in 14 years.

Tyler had served in the U.S. Senate, in the House of Representatives, three terms in the Virginia state senate, as governor of Virginia, and as vice president under William Henry Harrison. He was the first vice president to accede to the presidency due to the death of a president.

During his term in office, Tyler signed a trade and peace agreement with China (1844) and approved the annexation of Texas (1845). Florida was also admitted to the Union (1845).

John Tyler retired to his plantation, Sherwood Forest, near Richmond, Virginia, with his wife. He returned to Washington briefly in February 1861, to attempt a compromise between the North and the South prior to the Civil War. The effort failed, and Tyler urged Virginia to secede. He was preparing to take his seat in the Confederate House of Representatives when he died on January 18, 1862, at the age of 71.

Suggested Activities/Extensions

1. In 1843, President Tyler signed an act that granted Samuel Morse $30,000 to connect Baltimore and Washington with telegraph wires. Research to learn more about the invention of the telegraph and Morse code. How did life in America change after this improvement in communication? Use a map to estimate the distance between the two cities.

2. During Tyler's presidency, thousands of settlers headed west on the Oregon Trail. It stretched about 2,000 miles from Independence, Missouri, to Willamette Valley, Oregon. The settlers traveled only 12 miles a day in covered wagons. Answer these questions:

   ## The Oregon Trail

   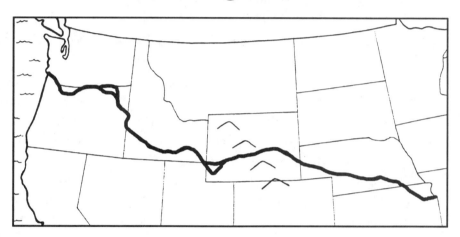

   - About how long did the trip take at this rate?

   - If they traveled from 5:00 A.M.–5:00 P.M., what is the rate per hour?

   Make pictures of the settlers, their animals, and wagons. Write a story describing what you think life would be like on a typical day. What kinds of dangers would they have faced?

3. Julia Tyler enjoyed the social life in Washington. She was known as a wonderful hostess. What characteristics make someone a good political wife? What would Julia need to do to prepare a party? Plan a guest list, entertainment, and a menu appropriate for the time period.

4. During the 1840s, the United States welcomed thousands of immigrants from Ireland and Germany. Do research to learn where they settled. What contributions did they make to early America? What must an immigrant do to become a citizen?

5. John Tyler had more children than any other president. Would you want to be the child of a president? Explain. What would life be like for a child of the president then and now?

Related Reading

Early Immigration in the United States by William J. Evitts, Watts, 1989.

John Tyler by Dee Lillegard, Children's Press, 1988.

The Oregon Trail by Leonard Everett Fisher, Holiday House, 1990.

Young People in the White House by Don Lawson, Abelard-Schulman, 1970.

Growing Up in the White House

John Tyler had fourteen children who lived to maturity, more than any other president. He had four daughters and three sons by his first wife, Letitia. After retirement, he and his second wife, Julia, had seven more children (five sons and two daughters) in fourteen years. His daughter Elizabeth was married in the White House in 1842.

Here are some other interesting facts about the children of the presidents:

- Esther Cleveland was the only child born of a president to be born in the White House. Her father was President Grover Cleveland (1885–1889).

- Scott Russell Hayes, son of Rutherford B. Hayes (1877–1881), was six years old when he hosted the first Easter egg roll on the White House lawn.

- Tad Lincoln had a secret code with his father that would always get him into the presidential office, even during important meetings. President Lincoln (1861–1865) promised to open the door if he heard three quick knocks followed by two slow ones.

- Alice Roosevelt, daughter of Theodore Roosevelt (1901–1909), was married at the White House in 1906. When she found the knife too dull to cut her wedding cake, Alice slashed it to pieces with the sword of an army major.

- President Calvin Coolidge (1923–1929) did not have time to play baseball with his two sons, so his wife played ball with the boys on the White House lawn.

- The only child of a president to die in the White House was William Wallace Lincoln, son of Abraham Lincoln (1861–1865).

- Amy Carter, the daughter of President Jimmy Carter (1977–1981) was ten years old when her father took office. She often took books to official state dinners to read between courses.

- Chelsea Clinton was named after the popular song "Chelsea Morning." She is an excellent student and skipped a grade while in public school in Little Rock, Arkansas.

Answer these questions on separate paper.

1. Which child read books at official state dinners?

2. Who was the only child to die while his father was president?

3. Which child is named after a popular song?

4. What are the names of the two presidential daughters who were married in the White House?

5. How many children did John Tyler have?

6. Who was the first son to host the White House Easter egg hunt?

7. Who was the only child of a president born in the White House?

Write/discuss:

- What would a typical day be like for the child of a president?

- How would your life be different in the White House?

- What would be good and bad about being the child of a president?

James K. Polk

Presidential Term (1845–1849)

11th

James Polk was born November 2, 1795, on his family's farm in Mecklenburg County, North Carolina. He was the eldest of 10 children. His father was a wealthy landowner and planter. When James was 10, the Polk family moved to Tennessee where James' grandfather had purchased land and settled. As a boy, Polk was weak and in poor health. He could not endure the difficult life of a settler. At age 17 he was sent to Danville, Kentucky, to undergo risky surgery to remove gallstones. He survived and returned to Tennessee with improved health.

In 1831 he received his first formal schooling in Columbia, Tennessee. In 1816 he entered the University of North Carolina and graduated with honors. He went on to study law and was admitted to the bar in 1820.

James Polk married Sarah Childress on January 1, 1824. She enjoyed her social duties, although her religious beliefs caused her to ban dancing and liquor in the White House. The couple had no children.

Polk served as Speaker of the House and governor of Tennessee before receiving the Democratic presidential nomination (1844). His term in office was marked by the compromise with Great Britain (Oregon Treaty, 1846) which established the boundaries of Washington and Oregon and the Mexican War (1846–1848). With the signing of that peace treaty, the United States added over 500,000 square miles of southwest territory. Americans had achieved what many called "Manifest Destiny." The country now stretched from the Atlantic to Pacific Oceans.

Polk realized that the acquisition of California would open the ports of the Pacific. The promise of easy riches brought thousands of settlers to California in the Gold Rush of 1849. The cities of San Francisco, Monterey, and San Diego grew rapidly.

James Polk became ill with cholera and died on June 15, 1849, three months after his retirement. He was 53 years old.

Suggested Activities/Extensions

1. The discovery of gold in 1849 caused much of the country's male population to move to California. Read more about the Gold Rush and write a news article about the discovery. Draw cartoons of miners panning for gold or design posters that encourage people to go west.

2. Women's rights first became an issue during the Polk administration. At the Seneca Falls Convention, a group of feminists wanted to abolish the "domestic slavery" of women. Describe the rights the women wanted in 1848. How is the women's rights movement working today? How do you feel about specific women's issues? Collect newspaper and magazine articles about current women's rights issues. Summarize them.

3. As a child, James Polk was often ill and unable to do his tasks. He was diagnosed with gallstones and surgery was recommended. At the time there were no anesthetics, and surgeons did not sterilize their instruments. Polk could have died. Talk with medical professionals to learn how medical practices have improved since Polk's surgery. When were anesthetics and sterilization introduced? How might history have been changed if Polk had not lived to become president?

4. Polk was called "Young Hickory." Use a Venn diagram to compare/contrast Polk with another president and Tennessee native, Andrew Jackson.

5. After his election, James and Sarah Polk spent three days visiting with Andrew Jackson at his retirement home in Nashville, Tennessee. Later, they corresponded. Polk valued advice from the former president. Write a letter that Jackson might have sent to Polk about selecting a cabinet, the boundary for the Oregon Territory, or his policy of Manifest Destiny.

Related Reading

Boomtowns by Robert Shapley, Rourke, 1990.

James K. Polk by Dee Lillegard, Children's Press, 1988.

The Story of Gold at Sutter's Mill by R. Conrad Stein, Children's Press, 1981.

Manifest Destiny

With the signing of the Treaty of Guadalupe, July 1848, the Mexican War ended. The terms of the treaty follow:

1. The border between the United States and Mexico was fixed at the Rio Grande River.

2. The United States paid Mexico fifteen million dollars and acquired 500,000 square miles of southwest territory.

3. Mexicans in the acquired territory were allowed to remain or return to Mexico at any time with no loss of property.

4. The United States government agreed to pay claims against Mexico lodged by American citizens.

A Look at the Map

During the two-year Mexican-American War, the United States acquired new lands. The map below shows the United States after the Compromise of 1850. Research to find out about this compromise. Then compare this map to a current United States map. What states have been formed since the compromise of 1850?

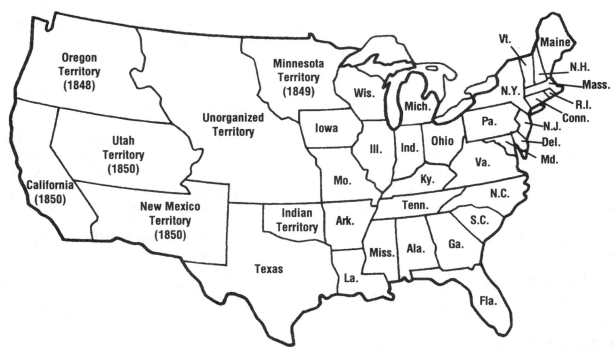

Extensions:

- How did life change after the acquisition of the new territory?

- What characteristics made James Polk a great president?

- Would you have wanted to participate in the Gold Rush? Explain.

- If you had been a Mexican living north of the Rio Grande, would you have stayed in American territory or returned to Mexico? What would have been the pros and cons of either decision?

Zachary Taylor

Presidential Term (1849–1850)

12th

Zachary Taylor was born on November 24, 1784, in Orange County, Virginia. Shortly after his birth, the family moved to Louisville, Kentucky. His father was a landowner and public official. There were eight children; only three lived to maturity.

Zachary received only a basic education. He grew up at the edge of the western frontier when settlers still feared attack from Indians. Little formal schooling was available to him.

He married Margaret Mackall Smith on June 21, 1810, in Louisville, Kentucky. She was religious and somewhat reclusive. It is said she promised God to give up social life if her husband returned safely from war. She also prayed that Taylor would not be elected president because she feared the changes to their personal lives. The couple had four children. By the time she became First Lady, Margaret was a semi-invalid and remained confined to her bedroom on the second floor of the White House.

Zachary Taylor was a career military officer from 1808–1848, achieving the rank of major general. He became a national hero after the battle at Buena Vista (Mexican War, February 1847).

Slavery was the primary issue of the presidential campaign. Taylor, the Whig candidate, was a slave owner who won Southern support easily; however, he was against the extension of slavery into the newly acquired territories.

Gold had been discovered at Sutter's Mill in California on January 24, 1848. Large numbers of people and prospectors moved west, and cities like San Francisco grew rapidly. The Forty-Niners risked a rough trip west in hopes of becoming rich quickly.

Zachary Taylor died in office on July 9, 1850. He was suffering from cholera and typhoid fever. He is buried near his childhood home in Louisville, Kentucky.

Suggested Activities/Extensions

1. Clay's Compromise of 1850 was the center of Senate debate at the beginning of Taylor's presidency. Henry Clay suggested admitting California as a free state, dividing New Mexico into two territories that could choose their own slave status, abolishing slave trade in Washington, D.C., and enforcing the Fugitive Slave Law which said free states must return runaway slaves to their owners. Discuss the seriousness of the slave question and choose students to debate different sides of the issue.

2. Zachary Taylor had little formal education. Although he was remembered as a good student, it is said he was always a poor speller. Learn to spell these words related to the life of Taylor.

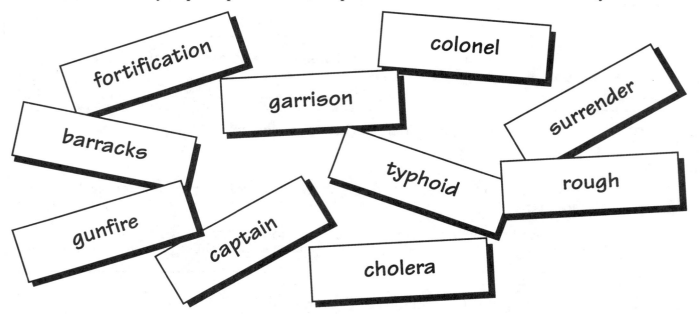

Write sentences that explain each word's meaning.

3. Dictate this passage spoken by Taylor on his death bed:

   "I am about to die. I expect the summons very soon. I have tried to discharge my official duties faithfully. I regret nothing, but I am sorry that I am about to leave my friends."

   Ask students to proofread the quote for spelling and punctuation errors.

4. Zachary Taylor died after eating a bowl of cherries and a pitcher of milk that were thought to be contaminated with cholera and typhoid fever. Research more about the diseases and the history of sanitation in our food supply.

Related Reading

Boomtowns by Robert Shapley, Rourke, 1990.

Zachary Taylor by Zachary Kent, Children's Press, 1988.

Zachary Taylor: 12th President of the United States by David R. Collins, Garrett, 1989.

The California Gold Rush

Zachary Taylor's administration helped guide the country through a period of enormous growth. With the discovery of gold at Sutter's Mill, more than 80,000 people ("the Forty-Niners") moved to California to seek their fortunes. Mining camps sprang up wherever gold was found. The miners were important to the development of the West. They helped establish permanent cities, transportation systems, and a strong economy. Many mining campsites have become tourist attractions in the western states.

Fact A—From 1837–1934 gold was by law valued at $20.66 an ounce.

Exercises

1. How much was the value of a pound of gold? _____

2. If there are 28.35 grams per ounce, what was the value of one gram of gold during this period? _____

Fact B—From 1850–1853 gold mining in California yielded $65,000,000 a year.

Exercises

1. If 80,000 people were involved in mining, how many dollars per year (on average) did each person mine? _____

2. What was the total dollar amount for gold mined during the above four-year period?
   _____

Fact C—The density of gold is about 1,200 pounds per cubic foot (19,000 kg per cubic meter).

Exercises

1. Measure your classroom to determine its cubic feet or cubic meters of volume. (Volume = length x width x height) _____

2. Using that volume, determine the weight of gold that would fill the room. (Weight = volume x density) _____ million pounds (or kg)

3. Using the answer in Fact A, Ex. 1., compute the gold value for the room. (gold value = weight in pounds x gold value per pound) _____ million dollars

---

Bonus: Compare your above answer to the value of gold taken by the miners in a year (using Fact B).

Extensions:

- How would the history of California have been different if the Mexicans had been the first to discover gold?

- Would you have taken the risk and gone to California as a prospector in search of easy money? Explain.

Millard Fillmore

Presidential Term (1850–1853)

13th

Millard Fillmore was born on January 7, 1800, in Cayuga County, New York. His father was a tenant farmer. Millard grew up as one of nine children, in the wilderness of New York. He helped with farm chores but always dreamed of a career of importance. Until he was 17, he had received only basic schooling in reading, writing, and math. At 19, he enrolled in the academy at New Hope. He was an eager student and married his teacher when he was 26 years old.

He was apprenticed to a clothmaker from ages 14 to 17 but later studied law and was admitted to the bar in 1823. Filllmore was an avid reader all his life and established the first White House library.

He married Abigail Powers on February 5, 1826, in Moravia, New York. She had been Millard's teacher and continued her career until the birth of their first child. She was frequently ill during her husband's term in office, and many of her entertaining responsibilities were given to their daughter, Mary. Millard Fillmore had two children with Abigail, who died in 1853. He married Caroline McIntosh in 1858.

He helped found the Whig party in New York and was elected to three terms in the House of Representatives (1833–1835, 1837–1841). Fillmore was vice president when Zachary Taylor died in 1850. Because of him, the Compromise of 1850 was passed, admitting California to the Union as a free state, defining the borders of Texas, and establishing the territories of New Mexico and Utah. The Fugitive Slave Act, the most controversial part of the compromise, returned runaway slaves who were residing in the North.

President Fillmore also sent Commodore Matthew Perry to Japan in 1853 to open trade with the Far East. He negotiated a treaty (signed in 1854) to open ports and guarantee humane treatment to American seamen on Japanese soil. That treaty brought Japan into world affairs and affected the course of history.

Because he approved of the Fugitive Slave Law, Fillmore was denied his party's nomination for the next presidential election. He retired to his home in Buffalo, New York, after leaving office in 1853. His wife and daughter died within 16 months of each other, and an emotional Fillmore planned a 13-month European vacation. While in Europe, he was notified that he had been nominated for president by the American Party. He accepted and returned to the United States in June 1856. He was not elected.

Millard Fillmore suffered a stroke on February 13, 1874, which paralyzed his left side. A second stroke ended any chance for recovery, and he died peacefully on March 8, 1874. He is buried at Forest Lawn Cemetery in Buffalo, New York.

Suggested Activities/Extensions

1. Millard Fillmore served as vice president under Zachary Taylor, but during the 1848 campaign he was ignored. He did not meet Taylor until after the election. How is that different from modern vice presidents? What are the responsibilities of the vice president? How does he relate to the president? Learn as much as you can about the position of vice president.

2. How is the job of a president different if he was elected than if he succeeds a president who has died in office? (Tyler and Fillmore were not elected.)

3. *Uncle Tom's Cabin* was written by Harriet Beecher Stowe in 1852. The book did much to convince people that slavery was a terrible institution. Share a copy of the book with your class and read aloud several passages. What effect did this book have on the slaves in the years to come?

4. The Fugitive Slave Act allowed slave owners the right to kidnap slaves who had run away to freedom in the North. The slaves had no right to a trial, and some free blacks were captured by mistake. Northerners resented the law. Abolitionist groups often posted notices about slave hunters in the area. Make an example of such a poster and/or write a newspaper article about the mistaken capture of a free black.

5. During Fillmore's presidency, the cost of postage was reduced from 5¢ to 3¢ per letter. Create appropriate word problems for your class, following these examples:

    *   How much did it cost to mail _____ letters before the reduction?
    *   How much did it cost to mail _____ letters after the reduction?
    *   How much money was saved with the new postage rate?
        _____
    *   Do research to learn more about the history of the postal service.

6. The Compromise of 1850 was established during Millard Fillmore's administration. Review the activities on page 41. Then have students complete the activity on page 47.

Related Reading

America's Vice Presidents by Diane Dixon Healy, Atheneum, 1984.

Millard Fillmore by Jane Clark Casey, Children's Press, 1988.

The Compromise of 1850

During Fillmore's administration, the Compromise of 1850 was an attempt to resolve the slavery issue and avoid civil war. A compromise is achieved when two sides in an issue agree to abide by the decision of a third party (arbitrator).

Complete this activity with three of your classmates; two students will take sides, and the third student will act as an arbitrator.

1. Decide on a problem. It may be a current event that you have read about in the newspaper or an issue of importance at your school.

   Write it here: _____

2. Determine who in your group will act as the arbitrator.

   _____ (name)

   The two remaining students in your group should accept opposing positions on the issue.

   _____ (name)

   _____ (position)

   _____ (name)

   _____ (position)

3. Brainstorm a list of possible solutions.

   _____   _____

   _____   _____

   _____   _____

4. With the arbitrator making the final decisions, decide on a resolution for the problem. Write it here:

   _____

   _____

5. All participants should sign to indicate their agreement.

   _____

   _____

   _____ (arbitrator)

Franklin Pierce

Presidential Term (1853–1857)

14th

Franklin Pierce was born in Hillsboro, New Hampshire, on November 23, 1804. His father was a public official and soldier in the American Revolution. He was a good student and easily passed admission tests for Bowdoin College at Brunswick, Maine. He studied classic languages, chemistry, philosophy, and mathematics. After graduation he studied law and was admitted to the New Hampshire bar in 1827.

Pierce married Jane Appleton on November 19, 1834. Their marriage was marked by sadness–all three of their sons died, leaving Mrs. Pierce depressed and reclusive. She resented her husband's political career and did not participate in the social activities of the White House. It is said that she wore black every day after the death of their third son.

Franklin Pierce served his country as a general in the Mexican War and as a member of the U.S. House of Representatives (1833–1837) and U.S. Senator (1837–1842). He was handsome and a fine public speaker. Because of his experience, Pierce was considered an excellent candidate for the Democratic presidential nomination in 1852.

He supported the Compromise of 1850 and wanted each new territory to determine if it would allow slavery. Because of this, war almost broke out in Kansas. These factors made him unpopular, and he was not asked to run for a second term as president.

Franklin Pierce and his wife retired to their home in Concord, New Hampshire, on March 4, 1857, after attending the inauguration of James Buchanan. The former president attempted in vain to console his wife, who was chronically depressed. When the Civil War seemed unavoidable, he delivered a speech (July 4, 1863) in favor of the South and warned that the government should not attempt to end slavery. His antiwar position made him unpopular in his native New England. He was denounced as a traitor, and his home was threatened. Jane Pierce died of tuberculosis on December 2, 1863. Pierce blamed himself and his career for her unhappiness. During the summer of 1869 his health deteriorated, and on October 8, 1869, Franklin Pierce died.

Suggested Activities/Extensions

1. Conductors of the Underground Railroad were actively helping slaves escape to the North. Read more about the movement and Harriet Tubman. Make a list of important facts learned and combine them into a story explaining the problem of slavery and describing how the railroad worked.

2. Workers laid 21,000 miles of railroad track during the 1850s. A transcontinental railroad was planned to run from Chicago to the Pacific Ocean. Senator Stephen A. Douglas invested heavily in the railroads. He knew that wherever the railroad went, business and success would follow. Explain this statement and discuss the importance of the railway system to the development of trade across the country.

Harriet Tubman

3. President Pierce wanted Japanese ports opened to American trading ships. He authorized Commodore Matthew C. Perry to take a fleet of ships carrying American goods to Tokyo Harbor in July of 1853. The Japanese were impressed with the merchandise they saw and signed a treaty opening U.S. trade and diplomatic relations on March 31, 1854. Why was this an important step in advancing the American economy? How does foreign (particularly Japanese) trade affect today's consumer? Brainstorm a list of things that students own that originated in Japan.

4. In 1853, the U.S. minister to Mexico, James Gadsden, negotiated the ten-million-dollar purchase (from Mexico) of land that is now Arizona and New Mexico. This completed the continental United States. Color a map of the country and label the states and territories.

5. Read more about the Kansas-Nebraska Act and the way it affected the balance of power between slave and free states. Write three to five cause and effect statements describing the situation.

   Examples:
   - Because Stephen Douglas owned land in Kansas, he proposed the Kansas-Nebraska Act.
   - Because Southerners favored slavery, they went to Kansas to vote for it.
   - Because Southerners and Northerners had opposing views, they had a terrible fight in the new territory.

Related Reading

Franklin Pierce by Charnan Simon, Children's Press, 1988.

Railroaders by Leonard J. Matthews, Rourke, 1989.

The Story of the Underground Railroad by R. Conrad Stein, Children's Press, 1981.

Kansas-Nebraska Act, 1854

Here are lists of free and slave states at the time of the Kansas-Nebraska Act. Add the state names to this map. Color the free states green and the slave states red.

Free States

California	Illinois	Ohio	New Jersey	Maine
Iowa	Indiana	Pennsylvania	Connecticut	New Hampshire
Wisconsin	Michigan	New York	Rhode Island	Vermont

Slave States

Texas	Louisiana	Mississippi	Florida	Virginia
Missouri	Kentucky	Alabama	South Carolina	Maryland
Arkansas	Tennessee	Georgia	North Carolina	Delaware

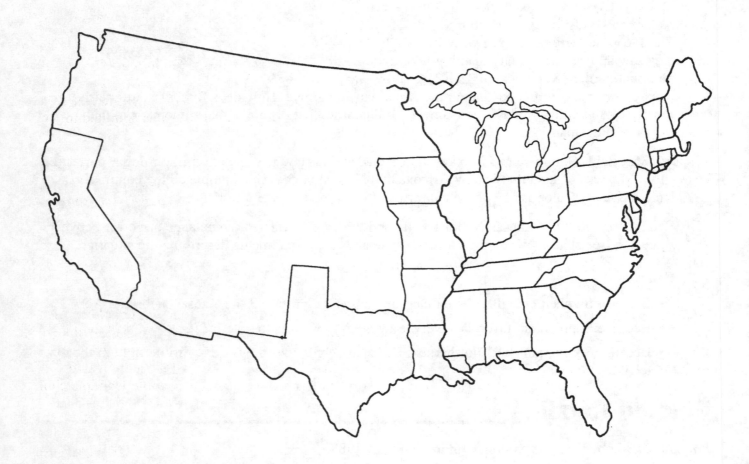

Bonus: What was Pierce's plan for slavery in the Kansas-Nebraska Territories?

James Buchanan

Presidential Term (1857–1861)

15th

James Buchanan was born on April 23, 1791, in a log cabin outside Mercersburg, Pennsylvania. His father, an Irish immigrant, was a merchant and farmer. He was the eldest of eight children.

He attended school in Mercersburg and entered Carlisle College. He is remembered as a discipline problem who probably would have been expelled from college except that the faculty had respect for his father. In December 1809, Buchanan moved to Lancaster, Pennsylvania, to study law. He had a special ability for putting laws into everyday language that people appreciated. He was admitted to the bar in 1812.

When he was 28 years old, James became engaged to Anne Coleman, the 23-year-old daughter of a millionaire, Robert Coleman. They quarreled, and she broke off the engagement. Shortly after that, Anne was found dead, possibly a suicide. A grief-stricken Buchanan vowed never to marry, a promise which he kept. He was the only president to remain a bachelor.

He served as foreign minister to Russia (1832–1833) and Great Britain (1853–1856), U.S. Representative (1821–1831), and U.S. senator (1834–1845). In 1856 he accepted the Democratic nomination for president.

Although opposed to slavery on moral grounds, Buchanan felt constitutionally bound to uphold it. He favored admitting Kansas to the Union as a slave state. Opposition to slavery continued, and by the time Buchanan was leaving office, seven states had joined to form the Confederate States of America under President Jefferson Davis. Buchanan felt that the federal government lacked the authority to force states to remain in the Union. He feared that confronting the seceding states would lead to a civil war. Buchanan declined to seek a second term in office because he was unable to solve the sectional differences that were leading the country to war.

He returned to a private retirement at Wheatland, his estate in Lancaster, Pennsylavania. He seldom commented publicly on current events but supported the Union and Abraham Lincoln. He died of pneumonia and heart problems on June 1, 1868.

Suggested Activities/Extensions

1. James Buchanan was the only president to remain a bachelor. He had been engaged to a woman, Anne Coleman, but she died before their marriage. Buchanan vowed never to marry. Instead, his niece, Harriet Lane, acted as hostess. How important is it to have a First Lady? What are her duties? Gather information about former (or current) First Ladies, their lives and activities.

2. In 1854, Buchanan (as minister to Great Britain) joined Pierre Soule, minister to Spain, and John Mason, minister to France, in writing the Ostend Manifesto. This document suggested that Cuba should be part of the United States and that it should be taken by force if necessary. The North vetoed the purchase, saying that Cuba would become another slave state. What is the status of Cuba today? How would life in the United States and in Cuba be different today if we had acquired Cuba in 1854?

3. The Pony Express service began in 1860 as a way to show that mail could be delivered promptly. It used a relay system and lightweight riders. The riders changed horses six to eight times before passing the mail to a fresh rider. They traveled 24 hours a day. Using this system, it was possible to move mail nearly 2,000 miles in ten days. The Pony Express lost money and went out of business. Could mail have been delivered in a better way? How did transportation and internal improvements speed delivery? Ask a mail carrier about time needed to send mail to various locations from your home. Learn what is the fastest way to send mail today.

4. The most important problem of Buchanan's time was slavery. He believed it to be "a great moral and political evil." Post this chart and add information that you have learned and will learn during your study of Abraham Lincoln.

Slavery Debate		
political	**economic**	**moral**

Related Reading _____

James Buchanan by Marlene Targ Brill, Children's Press, 1988.

Mail Riders: Paul Revere to Pony Express by Edith McCall, Children's Press, 1961.

Secession

1 **Activity:** Read more about Jefferson Davis and the Confederate States of America. List five facts that you learned about the Confederation.

   1. _____

   2. _____

   3. _____

   4. _____

   5. _____

2 **Activity:** Buchanan felt that the federal government lacked the authority to force states to remain in the Union. He feared that confronting the seceding states would lead to civil war. Do you think that Buchanan was a good leader? Explain.

_____

_____

_____

3 **Activity:** Choose another president you have studied and explain what you believe his opinion would have been on the secession issue.

President _____

Opinion _____

4 **Activity:** Use the map on page 50 (Pierce) to mark the states that seceded: South Carolina, Alabama, Florida, Georgia, Louisiana, Mississippi, Texas.

How did the secession of these states affect the Northern economy?

_____

_____

_____

_____

Section 2

Emancipation and Reconstruction

In the South many people believed that loyalty to their particular state was more important than loyalty to the Union. The Southern cotton plantations relied on slave labor, while the North was becoming industrialized and believed that slavery was wrong. Politicians could not agree on whether new states should permit slavery. It was this conflict between two basic ways of life that led to the start of the Civil War.

Soon after the election of Abraham Lincoln in 1860, the state of South Carolina seceded from the Union. Six other states, Alabama, Florida, Georgia, Louisiana, Mississippi, and Texas followed shortly thereafter. They formed a new government, the Confederate States of America, and elected Jefferson Davis their president. Lincoln believed that no state had the right to leave the Union, but in an effort to keep peace, he offered to continue slavery in states where it was not already illegal.

The North was superior in both resources and manufacturing. It had control of shipping but still had a difficult time occupying the Southern states and ending the struggle. The Southern strategy was to make the war so costly (in terms of money and lives) that the people would want to give up.

The Civil War began when the South fired on Fort Sumter (which was federal property) in Charleston, South Carolina. The battle ended with a Union surrender, though there were no soldiers killed on either side. Shortly after that, four more slave states, Arkansas, Tenneessee, North Carolina, and Virginia, joined the Confederacy. General Robert E. Lee was commander in chief of all the Confederate forces. In 1864, Brigadier General Ulysses S. Grant was made general in chief of all the Union armies.

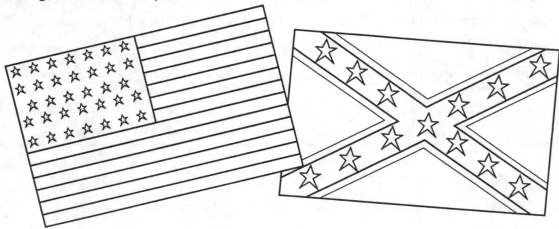

54

Emancipation and Reconstruction

(cont.)

The land and sea battles claimed about one million lives. After the Union victory at Antietam (1863), Lincoln issued the Emancipation Proclamation that declared slaves in the Southern states were free. (They actually were not freed until the war was over in 1865.) Another important Union victory was at Gettysburg, Pennsylvania, where Lincoln delivered his famous Gettysburg Address (page 59).

Lee surrendered to Grant April 9, 1865, at Appomattox Court House after defeats at Vicksburg, Richmond, and Petersburg. Five days later, Abraham Lincoln was assassinated by a Southern sympathizer, John Wilkes Booth, while watching a play at Ford's Theatre in Washington.

After Lincoln's death, a plan for reconstruction was undertaken by Andrew Johnson, the new president. It was most important to reunite the states. The states had to approve the Thirteenth Amendment, which abolished slavery. By the end of 1865, all the Confederate states (but Texas) had reentered the Union. In March 1865, Congress established the Freedmen's Bureau to provide freed slaves with food and medical care. They also set up schools and helped former slaves find jobs. Slaves could be legally married, and their children belonged to them, not the slave owner.

The South was ruled by the Union army until it formed new state governments. The new state legislatures had to adopt two new amendments to the Constitution. The Fourteenth Amendment said all people born in the United States were citizens and would be treated equally under the law. The Fifteenth Amendment said no citizen could be denied the right to vote, regardless of color or race. Southerners were unhappy with the changes.

Many Southerners did not like to see blacks holding public office and voting. To control blacks, some people turned to violence. Sometimes they hid the polling places or did not count black votes. In 1877 the Union soldiers finally left the South. Reconstruction was over. Soon the white Southerners regained control of their state governments. They moved the South toward complete segregation.

Emancipation and Reconstruction

(cont.)

Name/Dates	Political Party	State	Achievements/Events
Abraham Lincoln (1809–1865)	Republican	Illinois	Civil War
Andrew Johnson (1808–1875)	Democrat	North Carolina	Reconstruction, purchased Alaska, impeachment
Ulysses S. Grant (1822–1885)	Republican	Ohio	Specie Act, Reconstruction
Rutherford B. Hayes (1822–1893)	Republican	Ohio	Civil Service, reform, Treaty of 1880, Panama Canal policy speech
James A. Garfield (1831–1881)	Republican	Ohio	assassination
Chester A. Arthur (1829–1886)	Republican	Vermont	Mongrel Tariff, Pendleton Act
Grover Cleveland (1837–1908)	Democrat	New Jersey	depression, against protective tariff, Dawes Severalty Act (1887)
Benjamin Harrison (1833–1901)	Republican	Ohio	Sherman Antitrust Act (1890), six new states
William McKinley (1843–1901)	Republican	Ohio	Spanish-American War, annex Hawaii, open trade with China

Abraham Lincoln

Presidential Term (1861–1865)

16th

Abraham Lincoln was born February 12, 1809, in a log cabin in the backwoods of Kentucky. When he was seven years old, his family moved to southwest Indiana where Lincoln helped to clear the fields and plant crops. His mother died when he was nine years old and his father remarried about a year later. He got along well with his stepmother and her three children. The family made another move to Illinois in 1830. Abraham was 21 years old and six feet four inches tall. He was muscular and physically powerful.

Abraham once said he went to school by "the littles"—a little now and a little then. He enjoyed reading and was a self-taught prairie lawyer. His political future began to take shape with his successful legal career in Springfield, Illinois. He ran for public office several times and served in the Illinois legislature and as a member of the U.S. House of Representatives.

He married Mary Todd on November 4, 1842. They had four children, Robert (the only one who lived to adulthood), Edward, William, and Thomas ("Tad").

In 1858 he was the Republican candidate for the Senate. Though he was not an abolitionist, he was morally against slavery, a practice he had seen years before while visiting New Orleans. He ran against Stephen Douglas, and though he did not win, their debates made him famous. He was devoted to the cause of personal freedom for all people.

In 1860 Abraham Lincoln was elected president of the United States. As expected, the Southern (slave) states withdrew from the Union and formed the Confederate States of America. He led the North through the Civil War and wrote the Emancipation Proclamation, freeing the slaves. At Gettysburg, he gave one of his most famous speeches, declaring that government "of the people, by the people, for the people, shall not perish from the earth."

The war ended just as he was beginning his second term as president. He was planning the reconstruction of the United States. Within days of his second inauguration, Lincoln was assassinated by John Wilkes Booth. He died early on the morning of April 15, 1865.

Suggested Activities/Extensions

1. Lincoln was born in Kentucky. He moved to Indiana at age seven. At 17 he built a flatboat and ran farm products down the Mississippi River to New Orleans. He married Mary Todd at her sister's home in Springfield, Illinois. He was named the Republican presidential candidate in Chicago, Illinois, and delivered his most famous speech at the battlefield cemetery in Gettysburg, Pennsylvania. He was assassinated at Ford's Theatre in Washington, D.C. Locate and label these locations on a map of the United States.

2. Lincoln was more interested in preserving the Union than ending slavery. Discuss the arguments for and against secession.

3. Make a list of words that describe Abraham Lincoln, his appearance and personality. Organize them into a character sketch.

4. Read more information about the Confederacy and the Union. What were the strengths and weaknesses of each group? Make a chart to show what you learn. Compare the advantages of the North and South. Which group do you think seemed likely to win?

5. Add more ideas to the slavery debate chart (started for James Buchanan). If you wish, have two students adopt opposing views and role-play an oral debate.

6. Do research to learn the major battles of the Civil War. Locate and label them on a map of the United States. Indicate which side was victorious in each.

7. As a result of the war, Clara Barton founded the American Red Cross to help people in need. What duties do women perform (then and now) in time of war? How does the Red Cross respond to disasters today? What can you do to contribute to the organization?

Related Reading

Abraham Lincoln by Jim Hargrove, Children's Press, 1988.

The Civil War by Philip Clark, Marshall Cavendish, 1988.

Clara Barton by Liz Sonneborn, Chelsea, 1992.

Honest Abe by Edith Kunhardt, Greenwillow, 1993.

Lincoln: A Photobiography by Russell Freedman, Ticknor, 1987.

The Gettysburg Address

Here is the text for Lincoln's most famous speech. It is inscribed in the granite walls of the Lincoln Memorial in Washington, D.C.

"Fourscore and seven years ago our fathers brought forth on this continent a new nation, conceived in liberty and dedicated to the proposition that all men are created equal.

Now we are engaged in a great civil war, testing whether that nation or any nation so conceived and so dedicated can long endure. We are met on a great battlefield of that war. We have come to dedicate a portion of that field as a final resting place for those who gave their lives that that nation might live. It is altogether fitting and proper that we should do this. But in a larger sense, we cannot dedicate, we cannot consecrate, we cannot hallow this ground. The brave men living and dead who struggled here have consecrated it far beyond our poor power to add or detract. The world will little note nor long remember what we say here, but it can never forget what they did here. It is for us the living rather to be dedicated here to the unfinished work which they who fought here have thus far so nobly advanced. It is rather for us to be here dedicated to the great task remaining before us—that from these honored dead we take increased devotion to that cause for which they gave the last full measure of devotion— that we here highly resolve that these dead shall not have died in vain, that this nation under God shall have a new birth of freedom, and that government of the people, by the people, for the people, shall not perish from the earth."

Substitute words or phrases that have the same meanings as the underlined phrases.

1. Fourscore and seven years ago _____

2. new nation _____

3. great battlefield _____

4. final resting place _____

5. fitting and proper _____

6. what they did here _____

7. unfinished work _____

8. thus far so nobly advanced _____

9. cause _____

10. shall not have died in vain _____

Andrew Johnson

Presidential Term (1865–1869)

17th

Andrew Johnson was born December 29, 1808, in a log cabin in Raleigh, North Carolina. His father died when he was three years old, and Andrew's mother had to take in work as a weaver and spinner to earn a living. When he was 14 years old, his mother apprenticed Andrew and his brother William to a tailor, James Selby. Several years later, Andrew moved to Greenville, Tennessee, with his family and became the town tailor. He did not attend a single day of formal schooling. He taught himself to read.

He was married to Eliza McCardle on May 17, 1827. She was only 16 years old. The couple met when Johnson's family moved to Greenville. She was educated and tutored Andrew in writing, reading, mathematics, and spelling. In middle age, Eliza became ill and though she was present in the White House, she was unable to perform her duties as First Lady. The couple had five children, all born in Greenville, Tennessee.

Johnson was the governor of Tennessee (1853–1857) and a U.S. Senator (1857–1862). As the Civil War loomed, he was the only Southern senator to uphold the Union, and when Tennessee seceded, he split with his state. He was regarded as a traitor to the South, and for awhile, his life was threatened. He was the Democratic vice-presidential candidate chosen by Republicans under a Republican president, Abraham Lincoln, in an effort to balance the ticket.

After Lincoln's assassination, Andrew Johnson tried to continue Lincoln's plan for Reconstruction in the South. He hoped to restore legal status to the seceded states and give blacks the right to vote, but Southerners had no intention of sharing political power with former slaves. Radical Republicans in the North wanted to be sure that the South would not return to its position of power prior to the war.

In 1868, the House voted to impeach President Johnson for "high crimes and misdemeanors." He was given ten days to prepare for trial and was acquitted by just one vote. This was the only impeachment of a president in U.S. history.

He remained active in the Democratic party after retirement and became the only president to serve in the Senate (1875) after leaving the White House. He died on July 31, 1875, after suffering two strokes. He is buried in Greenville, Tennessee.

Suggested Activities/Extensions

1. To discuss the job of a tailor, consider what they do, how they are trained, what tools they use, and the differences between a tailor and a seamstress. Look for tailors in your local phone book.

2. Do research to learn more about Reconstruction in the South. How do you think life on the Southern plantations changed after the war? Explain your answer.

3. In 1861 Johnson was the only Southerner who did not resign the Senate when his state wanted to secede. What do you think people in the North thought of him? How did his position on secession help gain him the vice-presidential nomination?

4. Brainstorm ideas about how history (and Johnson's political career) might have been different if Lincoln had not been assassinated. Would Lincoln have been able to carry out his plan for Reconstruction? Would Johnson have been nominated in 1868?

5. During the Johnson administration, the United States purchased Alaska from Russia for $7,200,000. Many people thought it was a bad idea. Read more about how and when Alaska became a state. Learn more about its native people. Make lists of the major cities, landmarks, manufacturing, and natural products.

Related Reading

Andrew Johnson by Zachary Kent, Children's Press, 1989.

Andrew Johnson: 17th President of the United States by Rita Stevens, Garrett, 1989.

A Child's Alaska by Claire Rudolf Murphy, Alaska Northwest Books, 1994.

Reconstruction and Reform by Joy Hakim, Oxford University Press, 1994.

Impeachment

Article II, Section 4 of the Constitution says, "The President, Vice President and all civil Officers of the United States, shall be removed from Office on Impeachment for, and Conviction of, Treason, Bribery, or other high Crimes and Misdemeanors." The practice originated in England as a legal way to begin criminal proceedings against a public official.

Impeachment is similar to an indictment from a grand jury, but instead of the case going to a jury trial, the House of Representatives conducts hearings regarding the charges against the accused person.

Then, if the House decides there is a good case, it will vote a bill of impeachment, which means there will be a trial. In the federal government, the Senate takes the role of the jury and votes to acquit or convict the accused person. If the person is convicted, even the president has no power to pardon him.

Constitution

Impeachment
- *Treason*
- *Bribery*
- *Crimes*
- *Misdemeanors*

There have only been two cases of the impeachment process involving presidents in the history of the United States. Andrew Johnson is the only president to have been impeached. At his trial, Johnson was acquitted by only one vote. The other case involved President Richard Nixon. The House of Representatives voted three articles of impeachment against him in July 1974, but he resigned from office before the hearings could begin.

Write a summary about what you have learned about impeachment. Use these questions to help you.

- What is impeachment? Where did it begin?
- What are some reasons that a public official may be impeached?
- What steps are necessary prior to an impeachment trial?
- Which presidents have been involved in impeachment proceedings?

Discuss:

- Why is it necessary to have special rules for removing public officials from office?

Research:

- Read more about the impeachment of Andrew Johnson. What were the roles of the Radical Republicans and Edwin M. Stanton?
- What was the Tenure of Office Act (1867)?

Ulysses S. Grant

Presidential Term (1869–1877)

18th

Grant was born April 27, 1822, in a two-room cabin in Point Pleasant, Ohio. When Grant was an infant, the family moved to a farm in Georgetown, Ohio, where he grew up doing farm chores. He hoped to be a farmer or downriver trader. Grant was an above average student who did particularly well in mathematics.

His father surprised him by arranging his appointment to West Point in 1838. His given name was Hiram Ulysses Grant; however, he did not like the idea of having the initials H.U.G. on his uniform. His name was changed to Ulysses S. Grant on his enrollment papers. He graduated in 1843 and became a second lieutenant in the infantry.

Grant met his wife, Julia, through her brother while a student at West Point. They were engaged for four years, during which time they saw each other only once because of Grant's military service. After his election, Mrs. Grant entertained lavishly as First Lady. Their daughter, Ellen, was married in the White House on May 21, 1874.

Ulysses S. Grant was a professional soldier, serving in the Mexican War (1846–1848) and the Civil War (1861–1865). He forced the surrender of General Robert E. Lee at Appomattox, Virginia, which ended the Civil War. He returned to the Capitol a hero and was given the rank of full general. He received the Republican nomination for president and easily won the election with the campaign slogan, "Let us have peace."

Though Grant was an honest man, his administration was marked by serious scandals involving the gold market, the Union Pacific Railroad, delinquent and stolen taxes, and bribery. The country experienced the worst depression (Panic of 1873) in its history.

Grant signed into law the Specie Act (1875) which directed the treasury to accumulate enough gold to redeem all paper money printed after January 1, 1879. This law strengthened confidence in the U.S. currency.

In retirement, Grant, his wife, and son toured Europe, Asia, and Africa. On his return, he became the first former president to be nominated for a third term. He chose to give his support to James Garfield instead of running again. In 1884, Grant was left bankrupt because of a bad investment in his son's business. He wrote his memoirs to make enough money to provide financial security for his widow. Ulysses S. Grant died on July 23, 1885, of throat cancer brought on by years of cigar smoking.

Suggested Activities/Extensions

1. In 1869, the first professional baseball team was organized in Cincinnati, Ohio. The Cincinnati Red Stockings were undefeated in the 1869 season. Learn more about your favorite team and/or players. Share baseball cards and information about their team statistics. If appropriate, write the rules of the game and make a diagram of the playing field and positions.

2. Alexander Graham Bell was granted a patent for his telephone in March, 1876. Discuss how this invention changed America and the world. What other inventions have had such a profound effect on society? How would your life be different without access to a telephone?

3. The Great Chicago Fire lasted for three days, from October 8–10, 1871. Nearly four square miles of the city were destroyed, including the downtown business district. How has fire fighting changed since the days of the Great Fire? Locate Chicago on a map and contact travel agencies to learn more about the city.

4. The Fifteenth Amendment (1870) said that citizens had the right to vote regardless of "race, color, or previous condition of servitude." Women were not given the right to vote until 1920 (the Nineteenth Amendment). How important is the right to vote? Why? Do your students intend to vote when they are of age? How does a person register to vote?

Related Reading

The Battle of Little Big Horn by Charles A. Willis, Silver Burdett, 1990.

This Is Baseball by Margaret Blackstone, Holt, 1993.

Ulysses S. Grant by Zachary Kent, Children's Press, 1989.

Unconditional Surrender by Albert Marrin, Atheneum, 1994.

Lee Surrenders at Appomattox

After the Union troops under General Grant captured Richmond, General Lee faced the fact that he would have to surrender. It marked the end of the Confederacy. It was the final victory of the Civil War.

The Generals met at Appomattox Court House, Virginia, on April 9, 1865, in the parlor of a farmhouse owned by Wilmer McLean. Lee was neatly dressed in the full uniform of his rank. Grant wore only a blue flannel jacket and plain boots without spurs. The only evidence of his rank were the stars sewn on his shoulders.

The two men agreed on terms as follows:

- Confederate men and officers would surrender.
- All Confederate arms, ammunition, and supplies would be captured property.

In an act of kindness, Grant offered:

- Confederate officers could keep their personal sidearms and horses.
- Confederate soldiers could keep their horses for farm work.
- Food was sent to feed the Confederate army.

Grant did not allow his soldiers to celebrate the victory, saying "The war is over, the rebels are our countrymen again." He chose not to shame the Southerners in defeat.

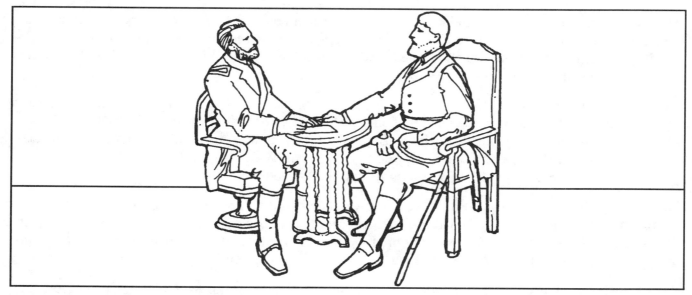

Choose one of the following assignments:

1. Write a conversation between General Robert E. Lee and General Ulysses S. Grant at Appomattox on the day of surrender.

2. Design a formal treaty showing the date, names of the parties, and terms of surrender.

3. Write a character study of Ulysses S. Grant. What character traits made him a great leader?

Rutherford B. Hayes

Presidential Term (1877–1881)

19th

Rutherford Hayes was born on October 4, 1822, in Delaware, Ohio. His father died 11 weeks prior to the birth, and his mother was left to support the family by renting out the family farm. Rutherford was very close to his older sister, Fanny, and his maternal uncle, Sardis Birchard.

He attended grammar school in Delaware, Ohio, and was remembered by his teachers as "industrious, well informed, polite, and respected by his peers." At 16, Hayes enrolled in Kenyon College at Gambier, Ohio. He graduated as class valedictorian in 1842 and entered Harvard Law School. He was admitted to the Ohio bar in 1845.

Rutherford B. Hayes married Lucy Webb on December 30, 1852, in Cincinnati, Ohio. Mrs. Hayes was the only First Lady to have graduated from college. She was a devout Methodist who banned all use of alcohol from White House social functions. Because of this she was given the nickname, "Lemonade Lucy." The couple had five children who lived to adulthood. With their mother, Fanny and Scott, the youngest children, hosted the first Easter egg roll on the White House lawn.

Hayes served in the Civil War (1861–1865), was wounded several times, and achieved the rank of major general by the time he resigned in 1865. He served two terms as governor of Ohio (1868–1872, 1876–1877) and became president in 1877 after a disputed election. His opponent, Samuel Tilden, won the popular vote, but Hayes was chosen by a 15-man electoral commission.

President Hayes believed in hard money and supported the Specie Act of the Grant administration. He encouraged civil service reform to assure quality federal employees and established the U.S. policy for building the Panama Canal across Central America.

President and Mrs. Hayes retired to their estate at Fremont, Ohio, after attending the inauguration of James Garfield. He continued to support Republican presidential nominees and was interested in black education, women's suffrage, and temperance. He suffered a heart attack and died on January 17, 1893.

Suggested Activities/Extensions

1. As governor of Ohio (1869), Hayes advocated sound money, equal rights for blacks, education, prison reform, and better treatment for mentally ill and poor people. What do these issues mean to you? Make a chart showing facts about each issue then and now. What has changed? What still needs to be done? How can individuals make a difference?

2. The phonograph and electric light bulb were invented during the Hayes administration. Use an encyclopedia to learn more about Thomas Alva Edison. Make a list of his inventions. Discuss how electricity has advanced society.

3. Hayes firmly believed that civil service workers should not take part in political activities. He wanted to end the "spoils system" begun during the Jackson administration. Brainstorm a list of civil servants. Categorize them according to area of service: federal, state, or local governments. Research the qualifications and requirements for positions of special interest.

4. In 1877, George Pullman produced a railroad car that was like a hotel room on wheels. President Hayes, "Rutherford the Rover," traveled across country in one of these cars to visit the peaceful Indians and California laborers. Make a drawing to show what the inside of the presidential Pullman may have looked like. You may also wish to design a dining car and meeting area for those traveling with the president.

Thomas Alva Edison

Related Reading

Almanac of American Government Jobs and Careers by Ronald Krannich, Impact Pubs., 1991.

The Civil Rights Movement in America 1865–Present by Patricia and Frederick McKissack, Children's Press, 1987.

Rutherford B. Hayes by Zachary Kent, Children's Press, 1989.

The Thomas Edison Book of Easy and Incredible Experiments by James G. Cook, Dodd Mead, 1988.

Inside the White House

During the Hayes administration, plumbing was installed in the White House. For the first time, running water was available.

A telephone, electric lights, and phonograph were other important inventions that were added during this period.

Suppose you were in charge of planning a state dinner at the White House. How would your job be made easier by these inventions?

If you interviewed these employees, what do you suppose they would say about the modernization of the White House?

the chef _____

_____

_____

the upstairs maid _____

_____

_____

the president's butler _____

_____

_____

the laundress _____

_____

_____

the president's secretary _____

_____

_____

James A. Garfield

**Presidential Term
(March–September 1881)**

20th

James Abram Garfield was born November 19, 1831, in a log cabin in Cuyahoga County, Ohio. His father died when James was just 18 months old. His mother struggled to keep the family farm. She had an unsuccessful second marriage to Alfred Belden. Garfield's mother lived in the White House during his term as president.

Garfield grew up in poverty. He became strong willed and aggressive in order to defend himself against the ridicule of other children. He worked his way through school as a teacher, janitor, and carpenter and graduated with honors from Williams College, Williamstown, Massachusetts, in 1856. He considered being a minister but decided instead on a career in teaching.

He taught classical languages at Hiram College and was president of the school from 1857–1861. Garfield studied law on his own and was admitted to the Ohio bar in 1860. He volunteered for military service during the Civil War and from that experience was drawn into politics.

Lucretia Rudolph became Mrs. James Garfield on November 11, 1858. The couple met as students at Hiram College but waited to marry until James was earning a living. They had five children who lived to adulthood.

Garfield served in the Union army from 1861–1863, rising to the rank of major general. He left the military to become a member of Congress where he served on the Military Affairs Committee. He was considered a radical, calling for the confiscation of Confederate property and the execution or exile of Confederate leaders. After the war ended, he became more moderate and supported Andrew Johnson in his plan for Reconstruction.

President Garfield was assassinated on July 2, 1881, by Charles Guiteau in the Baltimore and Potomac Railroad Station in Washington. He was shot twice, but neither bullet pierced a vital organ. He lay wounded for ten weeks and died of blood poisoning and pneumonia on September 19, 1881. He is buried at Lake View Cemetery in Cleveland, Ohio.

Suggested Activities/Extensions

1. Garfield is remembered as a gifted orator. Write a short speech on a current topic of your choice. Deliver it to the class in the style of a politician. Be persuasive. If possible, videotape the speeches to be critiqued at a later time.

2. Garfield conducted a "front porch" campaign for the presidency. This meant he stayed at home in Mentor, Ohio, and received small groups of people who came to pay their respects. He greeted each group, gave a short speech, and served light refreshments from the front porch of his home. How are presidential campaigns run today? Discuss the similarities and differences between modern and "front porch" campaigns.

3. Learn more about the medical benefits of sterilization, antibiotics, and x-ray machines. Discuss how these advances might have saved President Garfield's life.

4. Garfield's presidency lasted only 200 days (80 of which he was suffering from the gunshot wounds). As a state senator and U.S. congressman, he had been involved in many important issues facing the government. Garfield may have been a great president if he had lived. What do you think he would have accomplished? Explain.

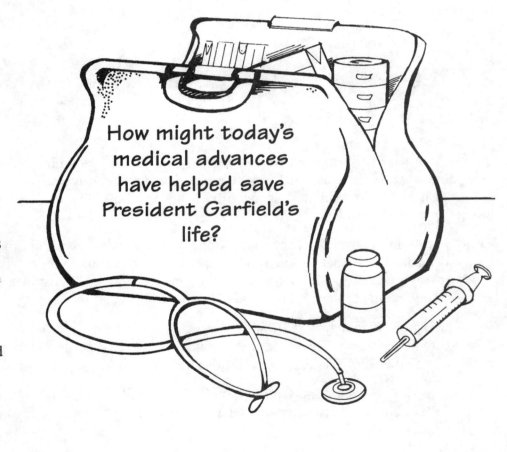

How might today's medical advances have helped save President Garfield's life?

Related Reading

James A. Garfield by Dee Lillegard, Children's Press, 1987.

So You Have to Give a Speech! by Margaret Ryan, Watts, 1987.

The Assassination of a President

Use this information to write a news article.

- Charles Guiteau shot President James Garfield in a Washington railroad station on July 2, 1881.

- Guiteau was angry because he had supported Garfield's election and expected to be rewarded with a political appointment.

- The president was shot two times, but he was not killed.

- The first bullet passed through his left shoulder, but doctors could not find the second bullet. There were no x-ray machines.

- Doctors did not understand the need for sterilization, and there were no antibiotics.

- Garfield's wounds became infected. He died on September 19, 1881.

- His body lay in state in the Capitol rotunda for two days.

(Headline)

(Photo)

Chester A. Arthur

Presidential Term (1881–1885)

21st

Chester A. Arthur was born October 5, 1829, in North Fairfield, Vermont. His father was a Baptist minister and abolitionist. Chester was the fifth of eight children, having six sisters and one brother.

After early schooling from his father, young Arthur enrolled in the Lyceum in Schenectady, New York. In 1845, he entered Union College where he graduated Phi Beta Kappa in 1848. He studied law and was admitted to the New York bar in 1854.

Arthur met Ellen Herndon through her cousin (and his friend), Dabney Herndon. The couple married on October 25, 1859, in New York City. They had two children who lived to maturity. Mrs. Arthur, who was often in poor health, caught a cold that developed into pneumonia. She did not live to see her husband become president. She died at the age of 42. Arthur's youngest sister, Mary McElroy, served as official White House hostess.

Some of Arthur's best work was as quartermaster general of New York state. It was his responsibility to clothe, feed, and equip the thousands of men who enlisted in the New York state militia during the Civil War.

After the war, he became involved with Roscoe Conkling and the Stalwart Republicans. Their candidate, Ulysses S. Grant, was the new president, and government jobs were given to people who had helped the candidate win. Arthur was made the collector of customs at the port of New York, a prestigious position with a high income. Then came an attempt at civil service reform under President Hayes. Arthur lost his job at the custom house.

Following the Hayes administration, Arthur ran for vice president with James Garfield. When Garfield was assassinated, Arthur assumed the presidential responsibilities with "tact and common sense." He established a three-man commission to set up a merit system for federal job appointments. This was the end of the spoils system. He passed laws to restrict the flow of Chinese immigrants, as well as criminals, convicts, and the insane, into the United States.

Arthur was ill with Bright's Disease, a fatal kidney ailment, and could not run for a second term as president. He retired to New York City where he died on November 18, 1886, of a massive cerebral hemorrhage. He is buried next to his wife at the Rural Cemetery in Albany, New York.

Suggested Activities/Extensions

1. The first hot dogs were introduced during Arthur's administration. A German sausage maker, Anton Feuchtwanger, first served them plain and later asked his brother-in-law, a baker, to make a roll to hold the sausage. Make a survey to find out how many hot dogs your students have eaten this week. Graph the results. Brainstorm a list of hot dog/hot dog bun brands at your local market and compare the prices.

2. The American Red Cross was chartered in 1882. Learn more about the history of the organization, its founder, Clara Barton, and what service it provides today. If possible, invite a volunteer to visit your room and explain the organization and its services.

3. Arthur attempted to limit the flow of immigrants into this country. Debate the pros and cons of such a policy as well as the effects of immigration on modern America. Do you believe there should be any limitations? Support your ideas with factual information.

4. Draw a political cartoon of one of these:

   - Charles Guiteau in jail

   - the end of the spoils system

   - immigrants being denied entrance into the U.S.

   - President Arthur eating a hot dog

   - Roscoe Conkling and the corrupt Stalwart Republican machine

Related Reading

Cartooning for Kids by Marge Lightfoot, Greey de Pencier Books, 1993.

Chester A. Arthur by Charnan Simon, Children's Press, 1989.

Chester A. Arthur: 21st President of the United States by Rita Stevens, Gannett, 1989.

Clara Barton by Cindy Klingel, Creative Education Inc., 1987.

Where Did Your Family Come From? by Melvin and Gilda Berger, Ideals Books for Children, 1993.

"Mongrel" Tariff 1883

Because of high tariffs on imports during the 1880s, the United States government had more money than it spent. The extra money was taken out of circulation and stored in vaults. This caused consumer prices to go down, and competition increased for the limited available money.

Chester A. Arthur set up a commission to study reducing the high tariffs imposed during the Civil War. The Republican Congress rejected the commission's recommendations for reducing tariffs and passed the "Mongrel" Tariff of 1883. It continued high protective tariffs favoring U.S. manufacturers. The Democrats favored a lower tariff to equal spending.

Answer these questions in complete sentences:

1. Where did the money come from that caused the Treasury surplus? _____

   _____

   _____

2. Why did prices fall during this era? _____

   _____

   _____

3. What actions were taken by the president to reduce the surplus?_____

   _____

   _____

4. How did each party respond to the question of high tariffs? _____

   _____

   _____

5. How might the excess money have been returned to the people?_____

   _____

   _____

Hint: Think about today's government programs like education, internal improvements, etc.

Grover Cleveland

Presidential Terms
(1885–1889), (1893–1897)

22nd/24th

Grover Cleveland was born March 18, 1837, in Caldwell, New Jersey. His father was a Presbyterian minister who graduated from Yale in 1824. Grover was the fifth of nine children in the Cleveland family.

When he was four years old, the family moved to Fayetteville, New York, where he attended the Fayetteville Academy. Later the family moved to Clinton, New York, and Cleveland enrolled in the Liberal Institute. He was a hardworking student but was unable to attend college because of his father's death in 1853.

Cleveland worked for a year as a teacher at the Institute for the Blind in New York City but discovered he was ill-suited for teaching. His uncle, Lewis Allen, arranged for Cleveland to study law in Buffalo, New York, and he was admitted to the bar in 1859.

Frances Folsom married Grover Cleveland in a White House ceremony on June 2, 1886. She was 21 years old; he was 49. Cleveland was a longtime friend of the Folsom family and had watched his wife grow up. Frances enjoyed life in the White House, and when her husband was defeated in 1888, she told the staff they would return four years later. She was correct in her prediction. Grover Cleveland is the only president to have served two nonconsecutive terms in office. He was both the 22nd and 24th president of the United States.

Cleveland established the Interstate Commerce Commission (ICC) to regulate railroad rates and put an end to discriminatory practices.

He led the country through its worst depression, The Panic of 1893, when thousands of people lost jobs, crops failed, and gold reserves dwindled. The president tried to repair the damage the Harrison administration had done to the economy by repealing the Sherman Silver Act, which had drained the federal gold reserves. He argued for a reduction in tariffs which had become so high that imports almost stopped (McKinley Tariff, Harrison).

Cleveland retired in March of 1897 to his home in Princeton, New Jersey. He enjoyed his children. Tragedy struck the family when his daughter, Ruth, died in 1904. To fill his time, Cleveland wrote and served on the Board of Directors of Princeton University. His health began to fail in April, and on June 24, 1908, he died of heart and kidney disease.

Suggested Activities/Extensions

1. Grover Cleveland's daughter had the Baby Ruth® candy bar named after her. Enjoy one in her honor. Brainstorm a list of popular candy bars. Make a graph showing your students' favorites.

2. An Atlanta druggist, John Pemberton, invented Coca-Cola® in 1886. It was intended to be a health tonic but soon became popular as a soft drink. The name was chosen because of the syrup's active ingredients: coca leaves and kola nut extract. Today it is the world's leading soft drink. Ask your students to estimate how many Cokes they drink in a day, week, month, and year and determine the cost based on 50¢ a can (from a machine). Later, determine the price based on the current grocery store cost for a 24-can pack. Compare.

Popular Products of the Time

3. In 1893, Cleveland was beginning his second term when he learned he needed surgery for a cancer in his mouth. He arranged for a secret operation so that the country would not be thrown into turmoil. Read more about the operation that was not revealed until 1917 in an article by one of the attending doctors.

4. In 1896, the Supreme Court upheld Jim Crow laws in the South, which said that separate accommodations are not necessarily unequal. The laws segregated restaurants, parks, theaters, and schools. Discuss the differences in life for black people then and now. What was done? What still needs to be done?

5. The Panic of 1893 lasted throughout Cleveland's second term as president. Railroads went broke, putting thousands of people out of work. Many of them became hobos. Cleveland did not propose any relief programs to help them. What is done today (by the government) to help people who are out of work? How is an area affected when a major business fails or moves away?

Related Reading

For God, Country, and Coca-Cola® by Mark Pendergrast, Macmillan, 1993.

Grover Cleveland by Zachary Kent, Children's Press, 1988.

Let's Visit a Chocolate Factory by Catherine O' Neill, Troll, 1988.

Now Is Your Time! by Walter Dean Meyer, Harper, 1991.

Cereal Becomes Big Business

During Grover Cleveland's second term in office, Dr. John Harvey Kellogg invented corn flakes (1895) as a healthful substitute for animal foods. He was a vegetarian and used the cereal in his sanitarium in Battle Creek, Michigan.

The first 10-oz. box sold for fifteen cents.

- What was the cost per ounce? _____

- What is the cost of a box of Kellogg's corn flakes today? _____

- What is today's cost per ounce? _____

- (optional) What is the percent of increase? _____

About the same time, C.W. Post, a patient at the sanitarium, realized the potential market for ready-to-eat cereals. Work with a few of your friends to do the following:

- Brainstorm a list of today's cereal brands._____

- Categorize them by manufacturer, Kellogg or Post._____

- Regroup them by their primary grain: oats, corn, wheat, etc._____

Read the nutritional information on your favorite cereal box.

- How large is a single serving? _____

- How many calories are in a single serving? _____

- How many fat grams are there? _____ sugar grams? _____

- How many milligrams of sodium are there? _____

List the vitamins present in your cereal. _____

Would you consider this to be a healthful product? Explain.

_____

_____

_____

Complete the following activities on separate paper:

- Make a list of words that describe the taste and appearance of your favorite cereal.

- Design an advertisement (or package front) for a new cereal. If you wish, work with your friends to prepare a commercial to share with the class.

Benjamin Harrison

Presidential Term (1889–1893)

23rd

Benjamin Harrison was born August 20, 1833, at the home of his grandfather, former President William Henry Harrison, near Cincinnati, Ohio. Benjamin's father was the only man to be the son of one president and the father of another. Harrison had three brothers and two sisters. His mother died before his seventeenth birthday.

Ben grew up on a farm, hauling wood and water and caring for livestock. In his free time he hunted, swam, and fished. He attended a one-room school near his home. His teacher remembered him as "the brightest of the family . . . but terribly stubborn." Benjamin was fortunate to have access to his grandfather's library. He was an intelligent student and an outstanding public speaker who graduated from Miami University in 1852. After graduation Benjamin studied law and was admitted to the Ohio bar in 1854.

Harrison married Caroline Scott on October 20, 1853. They had met as college students. They had two children. As First Lady, Mrs. Harrison renovated the White House, installing new plumbing and electricity. She put up the first White House Christmas tree in 1889. During her husband's reelection campaign, Mrs. Harrison caught tuberculosis and died. At age 62, Benjamin Harrison married Mary Scott Dimmick. She was a niece of the former First Lady. They had one daughter, Elizabeth.

During the Civil War, Harrison served as a brigade commander during the Atlanta campaign, making it possible for Major General William Sherman to advance on Atlanta. For his heroism, Harrison was promoted to brigadier general. He ran unsuccessfully for the governorship of Indiana but served as a Republican in the U.S. Senate (1881–1887).

Benjamin Harrison was elected president in 1889. Six states were added to the Union. Silver mining was big business in the West, and their senators wanted the government to buy silver from them. Harrison was concerned that a silver dollar lacked value but agreed (Sherman Silver Purchase Act, 1890) that the government would buy four and one-half million ounces of silver every month. The silver was not circulated as coins. The same year, the Republican Congress passed the McKinley Tariff Act which added an average of 48 percent to the price of imports. This nearly put some domestic industries out of business and turned voters against Republicans in the 1890 congressional elections.

Harrison's wife died just a few months before his retirement to Indianapolis. He resumed the practice of law and lectured at Stanford University. He died on March 13, 1901, after contracting the flu which developed into pneumonia, and was buried next to his first wife in Crown Hill Cemetery in Indianapolis.

Suggested Activities/Extensions

1. North Dakota, South Dakota, Montana, Washington, Wyoming, and Idaho were admitted as states during Harrison's administration. Mark those states on a map.

2. How do you believe Benjamin Harrison was influenced by his grandfather? How might his life have been different if his grandfather had not been president? Are you interested in following your grandfather's (or father's) career path? Explain.

3. As a senator, Harrison recognized the need for conservation and recommended setting aside land along the Colorado River for a national park. Years later, this area became the Grand Canyon. Collect tourist brochures and research factual information about the park.

4. On January 1, 1892, the government opened Ellis Island in Upper New York Bay as a processing station for Eastern and Central European immigrants. Research statistics for immigrants over the years and learn what is necessary to be granted United States citizenship.

5. President Harrison kept many pets at the White House to entertain his grandchildren. It is said they had dogs, horses, an opossum, and a goat named Old Whiskers. Do you know anyone with an unusual pet? Write about the care necessary for a variety of unusual pets, i.e., ferret, iguana, tarantula, etc. What are the negatives associated with owning an unusual pet? Contact several pet stores to determine the costs of various unusual pets.

Related Reading

Benjamin Harrison by Rita Stevens, Garrett, 1989.

Benjamin Harrison by Susan Clinton, Children's Press, 1989.

Coming to America by Katherine Emsden, Discovery Enterprises, 1993.

Ellis Island: New Hope in a New Land by William Jacobs, Scribner's, 1990.

Compare/Contrast

Compare/contrast Presidents William Henry Harrison (page 33) and Benjamin Harrison on the Venn diagram. Include information about each man's native state, military service, marriage and family, term in office, and death. In the middle section include similar information about the two presidents.

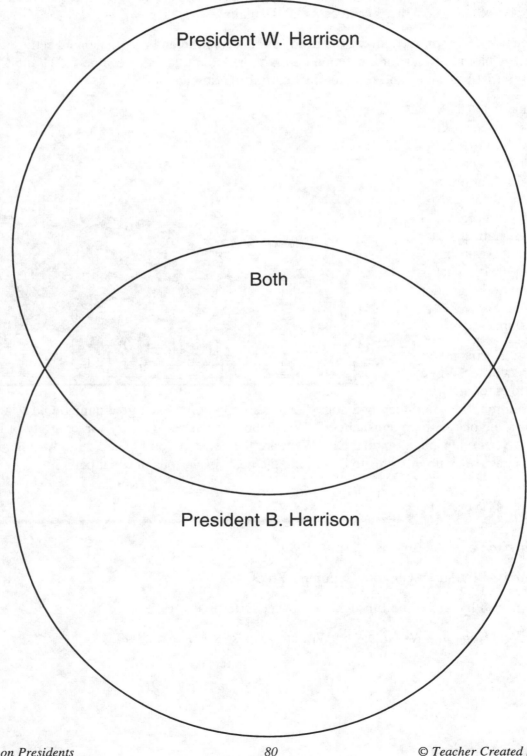

President W. Harrison

Both

President B. Harrison

William McKinley

Presidential Term (1897–1901)

25th

William McKinley was born January 29, 1843, in Niles, Ohio. His father was a pig iron manufacturer. His mother hoped her son would enter the Methodist ministry. William was the seventh of eight McKinley children.

He attended public school and the seminary in Poland, Ohio. His favorite subject was speech. At age 17, McKinley entered Allegheny College in Pennsylvania but could not graduate because of family finances and illness. After the Civil War, he attended the New York Law School. He was admitted to the Ohio bar in 1867.

William McKinley married Ida Saxton on January 25, 1871, at the First Presbyterian Church in Canton, Ohio. They had two daughters who died as young children. Mrs. McKinley was an invalid and epileptic who sometimes had seizures in public. The president was a devoted and caring husband.

At age 18, McKinley enlisted in the Civil War and served in the Battle of Antietam. He carried rations to the frontline troops. For his bravery he was appointed to the staff of Colonel Rutherford B. Hayes. After the war, he served as U.S. Representative (1877–1883, 1885–1891) and governor of Ohio (1892–1896). He was elected president in 1896.

In his first term, McKinley led the country through the Spanish-American War, giving the United States possession of Cuba, Puerto Rico, Guam, and the Philippines. In addition, he negotiated an Open Door Policy for trade with China. He wanted the United States to have equal opportunities with the other European powers already trading with China. McKinley was a popular president. He was easily nominated for a second term with Theodore Roosevelt as vice president.

His second term was cut short by an assassin's bullet. Doctors never located the bullet deep inside the president. They cleaned the wound, and for a few days, the president seemed to improve. He died eight days later, on September 14, 1901, of gangrene which had developed in the wound. Theodore Roosevelt took the oath of office immediately and promised to "continue, absolutely unbroken, the policy of President McKinley for the peace, the prosperity, and the honor of our beloved country." America had lost a beloved leader.

Suggested Activities/Extensions

1. McKinley worked hard as a member of Congress. When explaining his long office hours to his family he once said, "A good soldier must always be ready for his duty." What does that statement mean? Why did that kind of attitude make McKinley a good president? Apply the statement to your life. How would you change?

2. The Republicans restored a high protective tariff on nearly 4,000 imported goods. The average rate was 48%. Make a list of imported goods that you (or your family) have purchased in the recent past. Assign each one an approximate price. Add a 48% tax to that amount. What justification did McKinley give for supporting the tax? How would such a tariff affect your shopping habits?

3. The United States stretched from Maine to California, and the people were interested in extending the boundaries. The Spanish-American War lasted just 110 days and resulted in the United States taking possession of Puerto Rico, Guam, the Philippines, and Cuba from Spain. Cuba was granted limited independence. The Americans were happy to become a world power. Locate all the countries involved in the Spanish-American War and research the current situation of each government. Make a list of American territories and possessions today. Debate: Do you believe it is important for the U.S. to own countries around the world?

4. In a further effort to gain territory, the Hawaiian Islands became a U.S. territory in July of 1898. Do research to learn more about our fiftieth state.

5. In the late 1890s, the music of John Phillip Sousa became very popular. Listen to recordings of military bands playing *The Stars and Stripes Forever* or any of Sousa's other patriotic marches.

Related Reading

Cuba by Clifford Crouch, Chelsea, 1991.

The Last Princess: The Story of Princess Kaiulani of Hawaii by Fay Stanley, Maxwell Macmillan, 1991.

The Philippines by Emilie Lepthien, Children's Press, 1984.

Puerto Rico by Kathleen Thompson, Raintree, 1986.

William McKinley by Zachary Kent, Children's Press, 1988.

Campaigning for McKinley

Ohio businessman Mark Hanna organized McKinley's campaign for the Republican presidential election. People waved banners, shouted slogans, wore buttons, and passed out leaflets. Use the space below to design a button and a banner for William McKinley. Write three slogans or the text for a leaflet.

Slogans:

_____

_____

_____

_____

_____

_____

_____

_____

Section 3

World Conflict in the New Century

World War I

The assassinations of Archduke Ferdinand and his wife, Sophie, in June 1914, began the war which included the Allied Powers: Russia, Great Britain, France, and the Central Powers: Germany and Austria-Hungary. Italy entered the war in 1915, and the conflict eventually involved the vital sea routes and oil fields of the Middle East. In February 1917, German U-boats were ordered to sink all ships bound for British harbors. Five American ships were sunk, and U.S. involvement in the war seemed inevitable. War was declared on April 6, 1917. Men were quickly drafted and sent to help the Royal Navy hunt down the German U-boats. The U.S. troops under General Pershing proved to be a decisive factor in the victory of the Allied forces.

After several defeats, General Ludendorff felt that Germany could not win the war. He advised them to try to make peace with the Italian, French, British, and American forces. The war drew to a rapid close. In Germany, revolutionaries took over the government, and an armistice was signed on November 11, 1918.

The Peace Treaty of Versailles, signed June 28, 1919, established the independent countries of Poland, Czechoslovakia, and Yugoslavia. It also set up the League of Nations where countries could settle disputes in peace. Germany was excluded from the League of Nations and, left on her own, recovered from war and became increasingly hostile. Twenty-one years later the world entered another more horrible war.

The Roaring Twenties

In the Twenties, the country entered an era of prosperity. The confident feelings led to many social changes when the soldiers returned from the war. They were eager to get the most from life.

Prohibition was largely ignored as people made "bathtub gin" at home. Mobsters like Al Capone supplied illegal alcohol across the country to customers gathered to drink in secret saloons called "speakeasies."

Entertainment gained new importance for Americans. Audiences in 1927 were excited by the first talking movie, *The Jazz Singer,* and they cheered as Babe Ruth hit 60 home runs. In 1928, Walt Disney produced the first cartoon, *Steamboat Willy.* Women cut their hair, smoked cigarettes, and wore short skirts. The Charleston was the popular dance craze.

About half of America's homes had electricity, primarily used for lighting. Television was introduced to the public in 1928. Primitive roads made car travel difficult, so people traveled long distances by train. Charles Lindbergh's solo flight across the Atlantic Ocean on May 20, 1927, was celebrated with the decade's largest ticker-tape parade in New York City on June 11, 1927.

World Conflict in the New Century *(cont.)*

The Great Depression

In an effort to get rich quick, people invested heavily in the stock market. When President Coolidge left office he declared the market was sound, but in October 1929, people sold so many stocks that the market collapsed. Banks failed because they had invested heavily in the stock market. People lost their jobs. They had no way to pay their debts, so they were forced to sell their homes or cars. The country was thrown into economic chaos.

In 1932, one of four American workers was unemployed. There was no government welfare, so people were forced to beg or wait in breadlines at missions. Shanty towns (called "Hoovervilles" after President Hoover) sprang up in the big cities.

Farmers were unprepared for the drought on the Great Plains that turned the rich topsoil into a useless desert. Cattle choked on the dust. There was nothing for farmers to do but pack up and move west, hoping for work in the fields of California.

President Franklin Delano Roosevelt used the strength of the government to end the depression. His New Deal programs put people to work on internal improvements and building projects.

Gradually, the economy strengthened as Americans went to work, preparing for war. The Great Depression lasted for ten years.

World War II

America entered the war after the Japanese bombed Pearl Harbor on December 7, 1941. All men between 21 and 35 had to register for the draft, and women worked at factory jobs related to the war effort.

The Allies, Great Britain and the United States, were at war with the Axis Powers, Germany, Italy, and Japan.

Adolf Hitler had already occupied Poland, Belgium, Luxembourg, Holland, and France when the Americans came ashore at Normandy, France. The D-Day invasion was led by General Dwight Eisenhower.

From Normandy, the Allies swept through France and into Belgium, Holland, and Luxembourg. The Americans fought back the Germans during the Battle of the Bulge at the borders of Belgium and Luxembourg.

In the Pacific, General Douglas MacArthur prepared to retake the Philippine Islands. The Japanese suffered great casualties and lost many ships and aircraft, but they were not easily conquered. America could tell that Germany was collapsing, and they did not want the war to continue indefinitely. It was decided that two atomic bombs would be dropped on the Japanese cities of Hiroshima and Nagasaki. This marked the end of the war.

World Conflict in the New Century *(cont.)*

Name/Dates	Political Party	State	Achievements/Events
Theodore Roosevelt (1858–1919)	Republican	New York	Panama Canal, 1906 Nobel Peace Prize, Pure Food and Drug Act
William Howard Taft (1857–1930)	Republican	Ohio	income tax, *Titanic* sinks, direct election of Senators
Woodrow Wilson (1856–1924)	Democrat	Virginia	WW I, Federal Reserve Act, child labor laws, women's suffrage
Warren Harding (1865–1923)	Republican	Ohio	Teapot Dome scandal, civil rights advocate, League of Nations
Calvin Coolidge (1872–1933)	Republican	Virginia	Lindbergh's flight, Immigration Act
Herbert Hoover (1874–1964)	Republican	Iowa	Great Depression, Prohibition, veteran's bonus
Franklin D. Roosevelt (1882–1945)	Democrat	New York	WW II, New Deal, repeal of Prohibition

Theodore Roosevelt

Presidential Term (1901–1909)

26th

Theodore Roosevelt was born on October 27, 1858, at his family's home in New York City. He had two sisters and a brother. Theodore was a sickly child, battling asthma, frequent colds, and other maladies. His father urged him to strengthen his muscles by working out at a local gym. He began taking boxing lessons and developed into an avid sportsman.

Young Theodore was taught at home by his aunt, Annie Bulloch. He traveled abroad with his family twice, touring Europe, Egypt, and the Holy Land. In Germany, he studied the French and German languages. Theodore entered Harvard University in 1876 and excelled in science, philosophy, and German. He entered Columbia Law School in 1880 but did not graduate.

He was married to Alice Hathaway Lee on October 27, 1880. She was the next-door neighbor of his classmate at Harvard University, Richard Saltonstall. The couple had one daughter, Alice. Unfortunately, Mrs. Roosevelt died of Bright's Disease on February 14, 1884. Two years later, Theodore married Edith Carow in London, England. She was a friend of his younger sister, Corrine. They had four sons and one daughter. As First Lady, she remodeled the White House and arranged for the marriage of Alice, her stepdaughter.

Roosevelt was the governor of New York (1898–1900). He resigned to accept the vice presidency on the death of Garret Hobart. On the assassination of President McKinley, Roosevelt took the oath of office and was the youngest man to become president. He was easily elected president in 1904.

During Roosevelt's presidency, the United States got the right to construct, operate, and police the Panama Canal. He believed that the United States was obligated to help with problems in Latin America. In addition, Roosevelt brought suit under the antitrust laws against the railroad, beef, oil, and tobacco industries.

The Reclamation Act of 1902 set aside land for forest and wildlife refuges and provided for construction of dams to irrigate the West. Important laws were passed, assuring government inspection of food and drugs.

Upon retirement, Roosevelt took a year-long African safari (1909–1910). The members of his party killed several animals and collected plant and animal specimens for the Smithsonian Institution. Later, he took a similar trip to Brazil (1913–1914). On that trip he got malaria and had a gash on his leg which became infected. He never fully recovered from these problems. In January 1919, he developed mastoiditis (an ear infection) and rheumatism. He died in his sleep of a coronary embolism on January 6, 1919.

Suggested Activities/Extensions

1. Roosevelt enjoyed boxing, jiujitsu wrestling, horseback riding, tennis, hiking, swimming, polo, and rowing. In addition to rough physical activity, he enjoyed reading and kept a journal. What activities do you enjoy? Brainstorm a list of the favorite activities of your class members and show the favorites on a graph.

2. The teddy bear got its name from a cub that Roosevelt refused to shoot on a hunting trip in Mississippi. They have become a favorite toy worldwide. Bring several teddy bears to class. Write descriptive paragraphs about them. Draw a cartoon of the president and his cub namesake.

3. Roosevelt supported laws to guarantee sanitary conditions in the food and drug industry. If possible, visit a packing plant in your area. Notice the efforts made to assure the products are safe for consumption. Do research to find out the health hazards as well as penalties for noncompliance.

4. Roosevelt was the first president to fly in an airplane. The Wright brothers called their first glider the *Flyer I*. The first test flight was on December 17, 1903, at Kitty Hawk, North Carolina. Have you ever flown in a plane? Describe the experience. Would you have gone on one of the early flights?

5. In October 1908, the Model-T Ford was introduced to the American public. It sold for $850. If possible, locate a Model-T on sale and learn the price. Talk to the owner of an historical car to learn more about the hobby. Make a list of current Ford models and their prices.

6. Dr. Booker T. Washington, an educator, was the first black man to have dinner at the White House. What do you imagine they discussed? How do you imagine the staff felt about Roosevelt's guest? Role-play a dinner for all involved parties.

Related Reading

Conservation by Richard Gates, Children's Press, 1982.

Henry Ford, a Young Man with Ideas by Hazel Aird and Catherine Ruddiman, Bobbs Merrill, 1984.

How Teddy Bears Are Made by Anna Morris, Scholastic, 1994.

Nature in Danger by Mary O'Neill, Troll, 1991.

Theodore Roosevelt by Eden Force, Watts, 1987.

Theodore Roosevelt by Zachary Kent, Children's Press, 1988.

The Great Conservationist

Theodore Roosevelt had a lifelong love of nature. As a child, he wanted to become a zoologist. He was called the "Great Conservationist" because of his work developing natural resources. He used his influence to preserve nearly 200 million acres of government land in the Northwest and Alaska. In addition, he supported the Newlands Act (1902) which established 30 irrigation projects, including the Roosevelt Dam in Arizona. In 1905, he made Gifford Pinchot the chief of the National Forest Service. Pinchot oversaw the development of water power sites by private utilities. He also persuaded large lumber companies to adopt selective cutting techniques to save America's forests. Roosevelt's other contributions include: adding five national parks, including Yosemite and Mesa Verde, creating sixteen national monuments such as Muir Woods and Devils Tower, and establishing fifty-one wildlife refuges.

What does conservation mean to you?

Conservation is . . .

_____

_____

Why is it important to your future?

_____

_____

List three ways you can help preserve the natural habitat.

1. _____

2. _____

3. _____

Make a list of careers related in some way to conservation. What does each one do?

_____   _____

_____   _____

_____   _____

_____   _____

Discuss: Was Roosevelt's love of nature and interest in conservation incompatible with his interest in hunting and killing animals?

William Howard Taft

Presidential Term (1909–1913)

27th

William Howard Taft was born September 15, 1857, in Cincinnati, Ohio. Though his parents had hoped for a girl, he is remembered as an active, well-behaved child who enjoyed playing baseball. His father was a lawyer and a diplomat. "Taft" had two brothers and a sister who lived to maturity.

Taft attended public elementary and high schools in Cincinnati. He was a good student, graduating second in his class. He graduated from Yale University and the University of Cincinnati law school. He was admitted to the Ohio bar in 1880.

Helen Herron became Mrs. Taft on June 19, 1886. The bride graduated from the Cincinnati College of Music and taught school before her marriage. The couple had two sons and one daughter. Two months after moving to the White House, Mrs. Taft suffered a stroke which affected her speech. She never fully recovered but was able to entertain with the help of her sisters. Her greatest contribution as First Lady was the planting of 3,000 Japanese cherry trees in the Washington Tidal Basin.

Before election to the presidency, Taft was commissioner and governor-general of the Philippines (1901–1904). He was secretary of war under President Roosevelt (1904–1908). He supervised the construction of the Panama Canal. In 1905, Taft acted as secretary of state during the illness of John Hay.

His wife and President Roosevelt encouraged him to seek the presidential nomination in 1908.

As president, Taft enforced the antitrust laws, ending the monopoly of the Standard Oil Company. Taft's policy of Dollar Diplomacy was designed to bring financial aid to countries of Central America while protecting them from revolution and the possibility of foreign dictatorship. He encouraged U.S. bankers to invest in Nicaragua and Honduras. In 1912, he sent the Marines to crush a rebellion against the Nicaraguan government.

During his administration, the Sixteenth Amendment (1913) was passed, giving the Congress the power to collect income taxes.

After his defeat for reelection, Taft accepted an appointment as professor of law at Yale University (1913–1921). In 1918 President Wilson appointed him co-chairman of the National War Labor Board. He supported U.S. participation in the League of Nations. Taft served as Supreme Justice of the Supreme Court (1921–1930), writing 253 decisions in nine years on the bench.

When Taft retired from the Supreme Court, he suffered from heart disease and high blood pressure. He died in his sleep on March 8, 1930.

Suggested Activities/Extensions

1. Read more about the sinking of the *Titanic*. Make a list of the famous people who were on board. Research current safety regulations for passenger ships; compare them to the provisions on the *Titanic*.

2. Taft was the first president to later serve on the Supreme Court. How do you think his having been president might have affected his decisions? Brainstorm your ideas. Make a chart with facts about the current members of the Supreme Court.

3. Why are antitrust laws important to the economy? How would gasoline prices be affected if the Standard Oil monopoly had remained? Think of a way antitrust laws work for you as a consumer.

4. Taft's health problems (and his death) were caused by obesity. Throughout his life, his weight went down when he was happy and rose when he was under stress. Discuss the importance of maintaining a healthy weight, eating disorders, and a diet of moderation.

5. As secretary of war, Taft sent U.S. troops to support the government of Thomas Estrada Palma, the Cuban president. Palma resigned, and Taft served as provisional governor for a few weeks. Eventually, most of the rebels turned in their arms. Cuba remained an independent republic, and, in 1909, the American troops were withdrawn. Research the current status of the government of Cuba. Locate it on a map and discuss why America must be concerned with stability in Cuba.

Related Reading

Exploring the Titanic by Robert Ballard, Scholastic, 1988.

Ohio by Kathleen Thompson, Raintree, 1987.

The Story of the Powers of the Supreme Court by Conrad Stein, Children's Press, 1988.

The Tafts by Cassie Sandak, Crestwood House, 1993.

Titanic Crossing by Barbara Williams, Dial, 1995.

William Howard Taft by Jane Clark Casey, Children's Press, 1989.

Trust Busting

A trust is a combination of businesses that reduces competition or presents a threat of reducing competition. Today a more common term for trust is a business monopoly. During his presidency, William Howard Taft enforced the Sherman Antitrust Act (1890). This law said it was illegal to control the price or distribution of goods.

What is a monopoly? _____

_____

_____

In 1911, the Supreme Court found that the Standard Oil Trust was in violation of the Sherman Antitrust Act. The Standard Oil Trust was broken up because it unfairly controlled prices and restricted the oil business.

Suppose the two major soft drink companies merged. There would undoubtedly be changes made to reduce manufacturing and distribution costs.

How might the merger benefit the companies? _____

_____

_____

What might be the effect on the employees? _____

_____

_____

Explain why it is necessary for the government to control corporate mergers.

_____

_____

_____

_____

_____

_____

Woodrow Wilson

Presidential Term (1913–1921)

28th

Thomas Woodrow Wilson was born December 28, 1856, in Staunton, Virginia. He lived there less than a year when his family moved to Augusta, Georgia. His earliest recollection was of Lincoln's election and the beginning of the Civil War. Wilson had two older sisters and a younger brother. His father was an ordained Presbyterian minister.

Wilson was a poor student, having difficulty understanding arithmetic. He did not learn to read until age nine. He was weak and had poor eyesight. He got his basic education at home. In 1873, he entered Davidson College but had to drop out because of poor health. When he recovered, he entered Princeton and graduated with a 90 average. He studied law on his own and was admitted to the bar in October 1882. Later, he earned a Ph.D. from Johns Hopkins University in Baltimore. Wilson was the only president to earn a doctorate.

Wilson married Ellen Axson on June 24, 1885, in Savannah, Georgia. As First Lady Mrs. Wilson painted and drew sketches in a studio in the White House. She donated them to charity. She arranged the White House weddings of two of their daughters. She died of Bright's Disease in 1914. The president was devastated. Woodrow Wilson was married a second time to Edith Galt on December 18, 1915. As First Lady during World War I, Mrs. Wilson observed the federal rationing program. When the president had a stroke, she decided what matters were important enough to take to him. She retired with him and nursed him until his death.

Before his election to the presidency, Wilson had been president of Princeton University (1902–1910) and governor of New Jersey (1911–1913). He did not serve in the military.

Because the Republicans were divided between Roosevelt and Taft, Wilson easily won election. His most serious challenge came when the country entered World War I. Wilson set out Fourteen Points which he felt were necessary for a lasting peace. He led the American delegation to the Paris Peace Treaty for the signing of the Treaty of Versailles. He favored the United States participation in the League of Nations, a group intended to mediate differences among nations. He was awarded the Nobel Peace Prize in 1919 for his efforts to achieve world peace.

Wilson suffered a stroke while on a national speaking tour and had to rely on his wife to manage his work after that. The president and his wife retired on March 4, 1921, to a home in Washington, D.C. The former president tried to resume the practice of law but found it difficult because he was nearly blind. He suffered a stroke on October 2, 1919, that left him with slurred speech and a partially paralyzed left side. He never really recovered. Wilson died in his sleep February 3, 1924, and was buried without a state funeral.

Suggested Activities/Extensions

1. Wilson was the first president to hold a press conference. Brainstorm a list of questions about World War I, assign them to different students to act as reporters, designate a "President Wilson," and role-play a press conference.

2. The Federal Reserve Act (1913) established a system of 12 regional banks which were to serve as "bankers' banks." All banks who wished to participate had to deposit a portion of their capital at the Federal Reserve. The "Fed" then loaned money at a varying interest rate and was able to control credit. Invite a banker to your class to explain how this works on a local level.

3. The first income tax required a one-percent tax on all personal income above three thousand dollars a year. How much tax would you owe if you earned $4,000, $4,500, $5,000, etc.? How does this compare to current tax rates? What other taxes do Americans pay in addition to income tax?

4. The first modern art was exhibited in New York City in 1913. The most important works were in the style of cubism. Read more about Pablo Picasso and this style of painting. Make a cubist style drawing.

5. On returning from Paris, Wilson began a speaking tour of the country to explain why the United States should participate in the League of Nations. What do you think he said? Write a persuasive speech for the League of Nations. Some Congressmen believed that the U.S. should not be involved in any foreign problems. What would Wilson say to them? Debate the two sides of the issue.

6. During Wilson's administration, Congress passed the Child Labor Act (1919) to tax goods produced in factories that employed children. Learn more about working conditions for children during this period and how the situation was resolved. What do you think the government should have done about child labor?

Related Reading

Child Labor: Then and Now by Laura Greene, Watts, 1992.

Kids at Work by Russell Freedman, Clarion, 1994.

Picasso by Mike Veneziak, Children's Press, 1988.

Woodrow Wilson by Alice Osinski, Children's Press, 1989.

Woodrow Wilson by David Collins, Garrett, 1989.

Fourteen Points and the League of Nations

On January 8, 1918, Wilson gave a speech which set forth fourteen points on which to base a lasting peace after World War I.

The involved countries would agree to free navigation of the seas in peace and war, arms reduction of all parties, establishing equal trade among all peaceful parties, evacuation and restoration of occupied countries, and the establishing of a League of Nations, an organization intended to guarantee the political independence of all member nations. At the Paris Peace Conference, the "Big Four" (President Wilson, Premier Georges Clemenceau of France, Prime Minister David Lloyd George of Great Britain, and Premier Vittorio Orlando of Italy) drew up the terms for the Treaty of Versailles.

President Wilson was very much in favor of U.S. participation in the League of Nations. He toured the country, giving speeches to explain the importance of it to the American people. It was during this time that he suffered a stroke and became disabled. The Congress challenged the Treaty. Republicans did not want the United States to be obliged to intervene when countries around the world went to war. The United States never joined the League.

Discuss: How did the points of Wilson's speech help assure improved relations among countries?

Do you believe that the United States should intervene in world problems? Explain. How would you determine which problems to consider/ignore?

Answer: If you were to write a speech about how to achieve a lasting world peace today, what points would you make?

_____

_____

_____

_____

_____

Warren G. Harding

Presidential Term (1921–1923)

29th

Warren Harding was born November 2, 1865, in Corsica, Ohio. The family moved to a farm in Caledonia, Ohio, when he was a small boy. He was one of six children.

Harding attended a one-room school at Blooming Grove and went on to Ohio Central College (1880–1882). He took a part-time job at a printing shop and learned how to run a press. Because of this, he edited the campus newspaper while in college. He graduated from college (1882) with a B.S. degree.

Harding married Florence Kling DeWolfe at his home in Marion, Ohio, on August 15, 1860. She was a divorcée with one son. They had an unhappy marriage, but Mrs. Harding worked hard to make the family newspaper, *The Marion Star*, a financial success. She was interested in astrology and once visited a clairvoyant who predicted that her husband would become president but die in office. As First Lady, Mrs. Harding was an elegant entertainer. She died of kidney disease sixteen months after her husband and is buried by his side. The couple had no children.

Prior to the presidency, Harding served Ohio as state senator (1899–1903), lieutenant governor (1903–1905), and U.S. Senator (1915–1921). He was in favor of Prohibition and women's right to vote. On most difficult issues, he took the Republican position in order to bring unity to the party and avoid confrontation. He did, however, support Democrat President Wilson's efforts to keep America out of World War I. He was a strong patriot and championed the rights of the working man.

As president, Harding refused to join the League of Nations, thus assuring its failure. He signed papers ending the war without formal ceremony. Harding was the first president to speak for civil rights in the South. It was his hope that black men would regard themselves as "full participants in the benefits and duties of American citizens." He established the Bureau of the Budget, recognizing that there needed to be controls placed on federal expenditures. Finally, during his administration, Harding convened the Washington Conference for the Limitation of Armament in which Great Britain and the United States agreed to limit the number of battleships in their navies. In addition, the four powers, France, the United States, Great Britain, and Japan agreed to respect each other's territory in Asia and peacefully resolve any disagreements among them.

Early in 1923, Harding had to face rumors of corruption in his administration. Investigations proved that many of his appointees were corrupt. Harding began a speaking tour of the United States to convince people that he was still an honest man. He had high blood pressure and heart disease. While on the tour, he fell ill and died unexpectedly in San Francisco on August 2, 1923.

Suggested Activities/Extensions

1. By refusing to join the League of Nations, Harding assured its failure. What risks did Harding and the Congress assume by making that decision? What would you have done in Harding's position? Debate the pros and cons of the United States' involvement in the League.

2. With the development of the typewriter, more women entered the American work force. They no longer were limited to traditional women's work like teaching and nursing. What nontraditional fields are available for women today? What problems do they face in the business world? Make a list of the jobs held by the mothers of your class members. Indicate whether they are considered "women's work" or nontraditional jobs. Poll the girls in your class to find out their expected career choices. Discuss: How has the women's movement affected the workplace?

3. After the war, America experienced a wave of European immigration. Harding responded with the Immigration Restriction Act of 1921 which set the first immigration quotas in U.S. history. Indicate on a map of the U.S. where these immigrants typically settled. What factors influenced their choice of location? Do you believe there should be limits on immigrants today? If so, what should they be? Historically, how has this country benefitted from its immigrant population?

4. The prosperity and peace of the early twenties allowed people to enjoy life to the fullest. They were largely unaffected by Prohibition because of a network of speakeasies, night clubs where liquor was available. Read more about the "Roaring Twenties" and share information about the social changes that mark the period.

5. Design for President Harding's signature a document ending the war.

Related Reading

Early Immigration in the United States by William Evitts, Watts, 1989.

Ticket to the Twenties by Mary Blocksma, Little, Brown, 1993.

War, Peace, and All That Jazz by Joy Hakim, Oxford Press, 1995.

Warren G. Harding by Anne Canadeo, Garrett, 1990.

Warren G. Harding by Linda Wade, Children's Press, 1989.

Teapot Dome Scandal

Late in 1922, Harding learned of problems in his administration.

Charles Forbes, his friend and the director of the Veterans' Bureau, had skimmed the proceeds from the sale of surplus war goods and taken kickbacks for granting government contracts for overpriced goods. He was convicted of fraud, conspiracy, and bribery. He was sentenced to prison.

Secretary of the Interior, Albert Fall took an illegal payment of $400,000 for two tracts of petroleum-rich land which he turned over to two private oil companies. The land was the Teapot Dome oil reserve in Wyoming and the Elk Hill reserve in California. Fall was convicted of cheating the government and sentenced to prison.

As the Senate investigations were getting underway in 1920, Harding began a train tour of the country, called The Voyage of Understanding, to take his case to the people.

Investigations into these scandals were completed in October 1923, two months after Harding's death. It is possible that concern over his political future led to Harding's untimely death; however, there was never any question about his personal integrity. He simply made mistakes in choosing his friends.

Discuss/Write:

- Had he lived, what might have been Harding's political future?

- What could Harding have done to assure the loyalty of his friends? How do you think Harding felt about the betrayal? Did it contribute to his death?

- What should a president consider when making political appointments?

- Mark these cities of his tour on a map of the United States: Cheyenne, Wyoming; Helena, Montana; Spokane, Washington; Salt Lake City, Utah; Portland, Oregon; Denver, Colorado; Hutchinson, Kansas; Seattle, Washington; Idaho Falls, Idaho; San Francisco, California.

Calvin Coolidge

Presidential Term (1923–1929)

30th

John Calvin Coolidge was born in Plymouth, Vermont, on July 4, 1872. He dropped his first name after graduation from college. His father was a farmer, storekeeper, and member of the state legislature. As a boy, Calvin did farm chores and earned money selling apples and popcorn balls. In 1885, his mother died of injuries suffered in an accident with a runaway horse. His only sister, Abigail, died of a burst appendix at age thirteen.

In 1886, Calvin enrolled in the Black River Academy at Ludlow, Vermont, where he was an average student. He graduated with honors from Amherst College in Massachusetts in 1895. His best subjects were Greek, mathematics, and literature. He was admitted to the bar in 1897. It was during these years that Calvin Coolidge began his interest in public service. He was generally shy and sincere, not the typical politician; however, people trusted him, and soon he was elected to local office.

In 1905, Coolidge married Grace Goodhue of Burlington, Vermont. She was a teacher of the deaf. The couple had two sons, John and Calvin, Jr. As First Lady, Grace was a warm and entertaining hostess, often keeping the conversation going at White House dinners while her husband sat in silence.

Mr. and Mrs. Coolidge lived in Northampton, Massachusetts, where he was mayor (1910–1911). He was a state senator (1912–1915) and lieutenant governor of Massachusetts (1916–1918). As governor (1919–1920), he established a state budget system and improved working conditions for women and children and public employees. He attracted national attention when he called out state troops to control a strike by the Boston police force (1919). Coolidge believed there was no right to strike against public safety. He was vice president of the United States under Warren Harding and was sworn into office as president by his father upon Harding's death.

As president, Coolidge cut taxes and reduced the national debt by about a billion dollars. He also restricted immigration, vetoed farm price supports, and supported the United States' participation in the World Court. The Kellogg-Briand Pact, the Coolidge administration's greatest international triumph, used American influence to renounce war around the world.

On August 2, 1927, Coolidge announced that he would not seek reelection. After attending Herbert Hoover's inauguration, Mr. and Mrs. Coolidge retired to their home in Northampton, Massachusetts. The former president wrote his autobiography. He campaigned for the reelection of Hoover in 1932. He died quietly at home on January 5, 1933, after suffering chest pains and difficulty breathing. He is buried in Plymouth, Vermont.

Suggested Activities/Extensions

1. One of Coolidge's greatest sorrows was the loss of his son, Calvin, Jr., from a foot infection. The boy died when a blister on his toe developed into blood poisoning. How could that tragedy have been avoided? Learn about first aid procedures for blisters. What kinds of medicines/knowledge are available today that were not available in 1924?

2. As president, Coolidge was able to cut taxes and reduce the deficit. Why is it important to keep a balanced national budget? How are politicians attempting to do this? Look for news articles on the topic and work in groups to develop a budget plan for the future.

3. The Kellogg-Briand Pact (1928) was signed by fifteen countries who agreed that war was not the way to settle international disputes. Eventually, forty-seven more nations signed the agreement. It was effective until 1939 when dictators Adolf Hitler (Germany) and Benito Mussolini (Italy) took up arms to begin World War II. What is the best way to settle personal disputes? What are your school policies for resolving problems? If you sign an agreement, do you keep your word? Explain. Draft a sample contract to use in settling your next problem.

4. Read more about Lindbergh's solo nonstop flight across the Atlantic Ocean. Trace the path from New York to Paris. Compare/contrast the trip then and now.

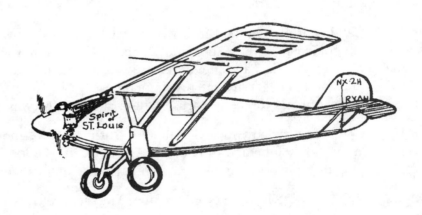

5. Babe Ruth was the most important sports figure of the twenties. In 1927, he hit 60 home runs for the New York Yankees and became known as the Sultan of Swat. Find out more about Babe Ruth and why he is considered one of the most famous baseball players in American history.

Related Reading

Babe Ruth: The Sultan of Swat by Lois Nicholson, Good Wood Press, 1995.

Calvin Coolidge by Zachary Kent, Children's Press, 1988.

Early Immigration in the United States by William Evitts, Watts, 1989.

Flight: The Journey of Charles Lindbergh by Robert Burleigh, Philomel, 1991.

Ticket to the Twenties by Mary Blocksma, Little, Brown, 1993.

Twenties Firsts

Here are some "firsts" that helped mark the 1920s. Write a sentence for each one that explains how or why it is important to you. You may omit any two items.

- adhesive bandages—1921 _____

_____

- cartoon—1928 _____

_____

- jazz—1920 _____

_____

- long distance telephone service—1921 _____

_____

- Miss America—1921 _____

_____

- nonstop flight across the Atlantic—1927 _____

_____

- permanent wave—1924 _____

_____

- radio station (Pittsburgh, Pennsylvania)—1920 _____

_____

- roller coaster—1927 _____

_____

- talking movie—1927 _____

_____

- television—1928 _____

_____

- zipper—1926 _____

_____

Herbert Hoover

Presidential Term (1929–1933)

31st

Herbert Hoover was born August 10, 1874, in West Branch, Iowa. He had an older brother and a younger sister. His father was a blacksmith and farm equipment salesman. When Herbert was six, his father died of a heart attack, leaving his mother to raise three children alone. Four years later, she died of pneumonia. The orphaned children were separated and sent to live with relatives. Herbert was sent to Oregon to live with his uncle, Dr. Henry John Minthorn.

After moving to Oregon, Herbert attended the Friends Pacific Academy from 1885 to 1887. He excelled in math. He was encouraged to study engineering at Stanford University. He was an average student and graduated in 1895 with a major in geology. He began work as a mining engineer with an English firm and was sent to Australia.

While at Stanford University, Hoover dated Lou Henry, the only female geology student. He cabled his marriage proposal to her from Australia. She accepted, and they were married in 1899. Soon after, the couple left for China where Hoover had been transferred. Mrs. Hoover was the national president of the Girl Scouts when Herbert was a cabinet member in the Harding and Coolidge administrations. As First Lady she was known for upsetting the White House staff with informal, spur-of-the-moment dinners. The couple had two sons.

As a mining engineer (1896–1914), Herbert Hoover moved his family around the world five times in five years. He made a fortune in the Bawdwin silver mine of Burma. In 1908, he formed his own company and developed important oil deposits in Russia. His work distributing relief food and supplies during World War I moved him into international prominence. He was the U.S. Food Administrator (1917–1918) and supported rationing as a way to save the country's resources.

Hoover was appointed secretary of commerce in the Harding administration and continued with President Coolidge. His solution to farm surpluses was to expand food exports and cut food transport costs. He did not believe in government farm subsidies. He easily won the presidential election in 1928. The stock market crash in October 1929 and the Great Depression which followed proved to be too much for the Hoover administration. His popularity with the public was destroyed, and he was defeated for reelection by Franklin Delano Roosevelt.

In retirement, Hoover worked for government reform in the administrations of Presidents Truman and Eisenhower. His health began to fail in 1962 when he was treated for intestinal cancer. He suffered a bleeding ulcer, lapsed into a coma, and died on October 20, 1964.

Suggested Activities/Extensions

1. President Hoover was a Quaker who supported Prohibition. We know that many people drank illegal liquor anyway and that it led to widespread organized crime. Debate both sides of the Prohibition issue. If you had lived in the twenties, which side would you have supported? Why? If appropriate, extend the discussion to the use of illegal drugs today.

2. Learn to read the stock listings in your daily newspaper. Compute the number of shares you can buy of five different stocks for $100 each ($500 total). Follow your stocks for one month. Compare your results with your friends at the end of the month.

3. If possible, talk with a stockbroker to learn how speculation and buying on margin are controlled today so that there will never be another Black Thursday.

4. Research the problems of farmers in the Midwest during the Dust Bowl period. What factors made the drought worse? What did the farm families find when they arrived in California? How do current farming practices assure that a similar situation will never occur again?

5. If available, watch a Marx Brothers movie made during this period. Notice how they make fun of rich people and discuss how movies of the day helped the poor forget their troubles.

6. Play a game of Monopoly, popular entertainment during the Depression. People who had no money for their own rent could "escape" by purchasing real estate with play money from the game.

The Marx Brothers

7. Listen to these songs of the Depression era: "I Got Plenty o' Nuthin', A Shanty in Old Shanty Town" and "Brother, Can You Spare a Dime?"

    How does music reflect social problems? Can you think of current examples?

Related Reading

Children of the Dust Bowl by Jerry Stanley, Crown, 1992.

The Great Depression by R. Conrad Stein, Children's Press, 1993.

Herbert Hoover by Susan Clinton, Children's Press, 1988.

The Great Depression

In the beginning, President Hoover did not understand the seriousness of the Great Depression. He was concerned about the people but firmly believed that government should not interfere with business. He saw the Depression as a normal part of a capitalist economy.

Hoover said, "I do not believe that the power and duty of the general government ought to be extended to the relief of individual suffering."

Do you agree or disagree with President Hoover? _____

Explain. _____

_____

_____

_____

What is the position of government on this issue today? _____

_____

_____

_____

_____

Hoover believed that voluntary cooperation and careful management would improve the situation. However, he had little success with the Congress, and his private efforts seemed to make the Depression worse. His administration provided no government aid to the homeless or unemployed; however, in 1932, it approved the Reconstruction Finance Corporation. The RFC loaned two billion dollars to financial institutions, businesses, and state governments with the hope that the money would filter through the economy and create jobs.

How could this best be accomplished? _____

_____

_____

_____

_____

Hoover was unable to gain the national confidence. People no longer trusted his administration to act in their best interest. He won only six of forty-eight states in the 1928 election.

Franklin D. Roosevelt

Presidential Term (1933–1945)

32nd

Franklin Roosevelt was born January 30, 1882, at his family's home in Hyde Park, New York. His father was a lawyer and financier. He was founder of the Consolidated Coal Company and director of the Delaware and Hudson Railroad. The Roosevelts enjoyed the privileged life of the very wealthy.

Franklin went to Europe with his parents several times as a child. His early education was with private tutors. At fourteen, he entered Groton Boys' School in Salem, Massachusetts (1896–1900), where he became interested in politics and public service. He later attended Harvard University and Columbia Law School. He was admitted to the bar in 1907 and began the practice of law.

Franklin and Eleanor Roosevelt were married on October 11, 1884, in New York City. She was his fifth cousin but was not from a wealthy family. Her mother died when she was eight years old, and her father was an alcoholic. As First Lady she became involved with important matters in government, helping her husband after he was disabled. She was very committed to helping the underprivileged. The couple had five children, four sons and a daughter.

Roosevelt was a New York state senator (1911–1913) and governor of New York (1929–1933). He was stricken with polio in 1921, which left him unable to stand without the help of braces. He won the Democratic presidential nomination in 1932.

The Great Depression was the most important campaign issue. Roosevelt assembled a group of advisors who helped him devise a plan (The New Deal, page 107) to assist farmers, businessmen, and the jobless. In winning the election, Roosevelt accepted the greatest challenge of his career.

As the only president to be elected to four terms, Franklin Roosevelt established diplomatic relations with the Soviet Union (1933) and a good neighbor policy toward the countries of Latin America. He led the United States' participation in World War II (1941–1945) and kept the American people informed of new government policies during radio "fireside chats" each Sunday evening. Roosevelt's first hundred days in office were the most memorable in history. He was a popular president who inspired a new confidence in the people.

Franklin Roosevelt died of a cerebral hemorrhage while vacationing at Warm Springs, Georgia, on April 12 in 1945. He is buried at Hyde Park, New York.

Suggested Activities/Extensions

1. Locate something in your community that was built or improved by one of the programs of the New Deal. Write a short paper explaining the project, why it was needed, and the jobs it provided.

2. Interview someone who lived through the Great Depression. Ask them about their memories of President Roosevelt and the country. Share what you learn with the class.

3. Read a biography of Eleanor Roosevelt and write a report explaining her contributions to the country. Design a character web that includes information about her interest in charities, civil rights, and how she supported her husband.

4. Design a character web for President Roosevelt. Include information about his family life, early career, and success as president. What characteristics made FDR a great leader?

5. Learn more about poliomyelitis, the disease which caused Roosevelt's disability. How was it transmitted and treated, and what vaccines have eradicated it? Read about the scientists who invented the vaccines, Jonas Salk and Albert Sabin.

Salk   Sabin

6. Rationing was an important feature of the war effort. Discuss with your students how they think people would respond to such governmental requests for belt tightening today. How would your life be different with four gallons of gas per week? two pounds of sugar a month? three pairs of shoes a year?

7. Franklin Roosevelt was successful with people because he knew how to explain things in simple language. Find examples from literature (or textbooks) and simplify them or use excerpts from Roosevelt's speeches, like "We have nothing to fear but fear itself," and expand them so they become more difficult to understand.

Related Reading

Eleanor Roosevelt: Fighter for Social Justice by Ann Weil, Aladdin, 1989.

Franklin D. Roosevelt by Alice Osinski, Children's Press, 1987.

Franklin D. Roosevelt: 32nd President of the United States by Miriam Greenblatt, Garrett, 1989.

The Great Depression by R. Conrad Stein, Children's Press, 1993.

V is for Victory by Sylvia Whitman, Lerner, 1993.

The New Deal

Here is a summary of the work programs advanced under Roosevelt's plan for economic recovery.

Civilian Conservation Corps (CCC)—This program put men to work in forests and national parks. They built roads and hiking rails, cleaned beaches and camping areas, and planted 200 million trees from Texas to the Dakotas. The trees were meant to hold the topsoil that was lost during the Dust Bowl.

Tennessee Valley Authority (TVA)—This project provided electrical power to the rural South by building a series of power plants and dams along the Tennessee River.

Public Works Administration (PWA)—In this program, the jobless built large-scale projects like highways, dams, and bridges. These workers built the Chicago sewage system.

Works Progress Administration (WPA)—Two million workers worked on improvements like rural electrification, flood control, and the building of schools and hospitals. This group built La Guardia Airport in New York. It also gave jobs to artists to paint murals on public buildings and writers to conduct research. A federal touring theater was formed to visit rural areas.

Roosevelt's plan for economic regulation also included the following:

Federal Deposit Insurance Corporation (FDIC)—This corporation provided federal insurance for bank deposits under $5,000 and now provides insurance for individual accounts up to $100,000.

National Housing Act (1934)—The act provided federal money for home loans.

Securities and Exchange Commission (1934)—The SEC regulates the stock market in order to avoid another crash.

Social Security Act (1935)—It provides a retirement income for those over 65 who have contributed to it.

Wagner Act (1935)—This act established the right of labor to organize and bargain collectively with unions.

1. In your opinion, which of these programs would be of the most benefit to the greatest number of people? Explain.

   _____

   _____

   _____

2. Which has the least value? Explain.

   _____

   _____

Establishment of a Modern Society

Franklin Delano Roosevelt died about a month before the war in Europe ended. The new president, Harry Truman, ordered the dropping of atomic bombs on the Japanese cities of Hiroshima and Nagasaki, forcing the Japanese to surrender shortly thereafter. America celebrated the end of the war.

Soldiers returned ready to marry and start families. This caused a housing shortage that led to faster and cheaper construction methods. Companies were producing appliances, automobiles, and clothing for an expanded market.

In 1946, British Prime Minister Winston Churchill expressed concern over Russia's continued occupation of Poland, Romania, Bulgaria, Czechoslovakia, Hungary, Yugoslavia, Latvia, Lithuania, Estonia, and East Germany. President Truman decided that the United States would come to the aid of any nation threatened by communism. This was the beginning of a Cold War between the U.S. and the U.S.S.R., which lasted more than 40 years.

The Korean War

In 1950, the United States intervened when the armies of North Korea entered South Korea. We did not want communism to dominate the world. Anticommunist extremists led by Senator Joseph McCarthy accused American citizens of communist activity. Some people were blacklisted and lost their jobs without proof.

A new, conservative president, Dwight Eisenhower, wanted to end the war. He did not want to risk a larger war with China. There was no winner. Korea was still a divided country. When Eisenhower left office, our country entered an arms race with the Russians. Both countries spent huge amounts of money on missiles, guns, and bombs.

The American people were still experiencing postwar prosperity. They moved to the suburbs and enjoyed television, modern transportation, vacations, and fast-food restaurants.

Segregation

Not all Americans were happy. Black Americans were still struggling for equal protection under the law. Even the Supreme Court decided that separate facilities (like schools and hotels) could be considered equal. Under the Jim Crow laws, even Native Americans and Alaskans were denied the right to attend schools or live in the areas of their choosing. Problems of racism were challenged and the "separate but equal" ruling was overturned by the unanimous decision of the Supreme Court on May 17, 1954. About this time, Martin Luther King, Jr., was emerging as a civil rights leader in the South. He was a minister who taught nonviolence and encouraged peaceful resistance to segregation. Large numbers of demonstrators participated in boycotts, sit-ins, and marches throughout the South. He also worked for the poor people in the country. On April 4, 1968, Dr. Martin Luther King, Jr., was assassinated in Memphis, Tennessee.

Establishment of a Modern Society *(cont.)*

The War in Vietnam

The United States next became involved in a war in Vietnam. The French lost the country (French Indochina) when the Japanese invaded during World War II. They wanted it back, but the new communist leader, Ho Chi Minh, aided by the Chinese, wanted to keep the country independent. America sent financial aid to help the French in Vietnam because of the communist involvement. The French were defeated and withdrew, but free elections were never held.

Many of the presidential advisors felt that we should fight in Vietnam. Our involvement started slowly with Presidents Truman and Eisenhower. Then President Kennedy sent much more money and many advisors. He was assassinated in Dallas, Texas, on November 22, 1963. Lyndon Johnson became the new president.

Johnson believed that America was winning the war when the North Vietnamese launched a surprise attack on the South. After the Tet Offensive, many moderate Americans no longer supported the war. Johnson announced a halt to the bombings and the beginning of peace talks. Today, many people believe that our involvement in Vietnam was a mistake and that the South Vietnamese people should have been allowed to fight for their own freedom.

President Nixon was a practical man who believed it was time to work with communist nations. He improved relations with China. He visited Moscow. Unfortunately, Nixon believed that he was above the law. His staff committed criminal acts against his political opponents. Nixon had to resign the presidency to avoid impeachment proceedings.

A series of national current events followed: astronauts landing on the moon, soaring gas and oil prices, Americans held hostage in Iran for 444 days. The national deficit grew at a rapid rate, and the Soviet Union, recognizing that communism was a failure, disbanded. Our country fought a powerful, short war in the Persian Gulf to support Kuwait against the Iraqi dictator.

Establishment of a Modern Society *(cont.)*

Name/Dates	Political Party	State	Achievements/Events
Harry S Truman (1884–1972)	Democrat	Missouri	atomic bomb, United Nations, Marshall Plan, Levittown, Korean War
Dwight D. Eisenhower (1890–1969)	Republican	Texas	interstate highway system, Civil Rights Act, Eisenhower Doctrine, *Sputnik*, U-2
John F. Kennedy (1917–1963)	Democrat	Massachusetts	Peace Corps, NASA, Cuban Missile Crisis, Bay of Pigs, Vietnam War, assassination
Lyndon B. Johnson (1908–1973)	Democrat	Texas	Watts riots, Job Corps, Head Start, Vietnam War
Richard M. Nixon (1913–1994)	Republican	California	Woodstock, détente, Watergate, women's rights
Gerald R. Ford (1913–)	Republican	Nebraska	Arab oil embargo, Nixon pardon
Jimmy Carter (1924–)	Democrat	Georgia	Peace Egypt/Israel, energy crisis, ERA, Salt II, hostage crisis
Ronald Reagan (1911–)	Republican	Illinois	Reaganomics, national debt, Iran-Contra affair, *Challenger* explodes
George Bush (1924–)	Republican	Massachusetts	end of Cold War, UN Earth Summit, Desert Storm
Bill Clinton (1946–)	Democrat	Arkansas	health care, AFTA, welfare reform

Harry S Truman

Presidential Term (1945–1953)

33rd

Harry Truman was born May 8, 1884, at the family home in Lamar, Missouri. His parents gave him "S" as a middle name to represent both his grandfathers, Anderson Shippe Truman and Solomon Young. Harry had one sister and one brother. His father was a farmer who died before his son became president. Harry had poor eyesight and needed to wear glasses as a young child. He did not participate in sports. At nine years of age, he had diphtheria which left him temporarily paralyzed.

Harry was taught to read by his mother. In 1901, he graduated from high school in Independence, Missouri. His favorite subjects were history and Latin. He was prevented from attending West Point because of his vision, so Truman enrolled in Kansas City Law School in 1923. Truman was a talented pianist.

He married his childhood sweetheart, Elizabeth "Bess" Wallace, on June 28, 1919. They met in Sunday school when he was six and she was five. Mrs. Truman was not happy living in the White House and did only limited entertaining. They had one daughter, Mary Margaret.

Before becoming president, Truman worked as a timekeeper for a railroad contractor, a bank clerk, and a bookkeeper. After volunteering for World War I, he owned an unsuccessful clothing store and haberdashery in Kansas City. He was a judge (1922–1934) in Jackson County, Missouri, and U.S. senator (1935–1945). As chairman of the Committee to Investigate the National Defense Program, Truman exposed waste in the military-industrial complex. Because of that, he was asked to serve as vice president during Franklin Roosevelt's last term.

When FDR died, Truman was not prepared for the presidency. He was now the leader of a country at war. It was his decision to bring an end to the war by bombing Hiroshima and Nagasaki. The United Nations, first conceived by Franklin Roosevelt, became a reality. Truman believed that the United States must intervene on behalf of any country resisting communism. The North Atlantic Treaty Organization was established to form a united front against communist aggression. Truman approved a plan to rebuild Europe after the war (1948–1952) and recognized the new nation of Israel (1948).

He decided not to seek reelection as president as early as 1949. The Trumans retired to Independence, Missouri, after the inauguration of his successor, Dwight Eisenhower. He remained active in political life until his death December 26, 1972.

Suggested Activities/Extensions

1. The United Nations was created during the Truman administration. Make a list of the member nations. Divide the class into groups of three to five students, assigning five countries to each group. List important facts and make a flag for each country. What is the purpose of the UN today?

2. Locate Hiroshima and Nagasaki on a map of Japan. Locate the countries of Europe involved in World War II. Mark them with small flags.

3. Israel became an independent state in 1948. Read more about Israel and Palestine and discuss the importance of this event in world history.

4. On his desk, Truman had two plaques bearing these sayings: "The buck stops here," and "Always do right. This will gratify some people and astonish the rest." Rewrite them in your own words. How did those sayings guide his presidency?

5. Between 1948 and 1952, the Marshall Plan provided twelve billion dollars for the reconstruction of Western European nations. How do you suppose the money was used? Do you agree with the American position of aiding countries defeated in war?

6. Divide the class into small groups. Present the following list of Truman's achievements to the class and have each group choose one achievement. Have groups pretend they are newspaper reporters of the time. Each group's assignment is to create a headline and write an article based on the achievement.

   - He is elected to the United States Senate in 1934 and reelected in 1940.
   - Truman represents the United States at the signing of the United Nations' charter in June 1945.
   - He signs the NATO treaty for mutual defense among 12 nations.
   - On March 13, 1947, Truman issues his policy for "containment" of Communism, later called the Truman Doctrine.
   - When the Soviets blockade West Berlin in 1948, Truman orders an airlift to the city. Constant shuttles keep the West Berliners supplied with food, coal, and necessities.
   - His Fair Deal increases Social Security benefits, raises the minimum wage from 40 cents to 75 cents per hour, and appropriates money for constructing low-income housing.
   - He fires General MacArthur after MacArthur publicly voices his unhappiness with Truman's refusal to allow a war with China.
   - Truman begins the fight to integrate schools.
   - He appoints the first African American federal judge.

Related Reading

The Buck Stops Here: A Biography of Harry Truman by Morrie Greenberg, Dillon, 1989.

Harry S Truman by Jim Hargrove, Children's Press, 1987.

Hiroshima by Laurence Yep, Scholastic, 1995.

Israel by Mary Jane Cahill, Chelsea House, 1988.

United Nations by Carol Greene, Children's Press, 1983.

Final Days of World War II

On April 25, 1945, Harry Truman learned that the United States had a new weapon of "almost unbelievable destructive power." President Roosevelt had authorized the secret "Manhattan Project" which produced a bomb that could destroy an entire city.

The war in Europe was over, and the Nazi government under Adolf Hitler had surrendered. Secretary of War Henry Stimson suggested that the atomic bomb would quickly end the war with Japan.

Truman met with Allied leaders in Potsdam, Germany, on July 16. On July 26, the Allied leaders sent an ultimatum to Japan. The Japanese ignored warnings and refused to surrender because they did not know about the A-bomb. Some scientists felt that the bomb should not be used to shorten the war; however, President Truman believed that if American soldiers would be saved, it should be used.

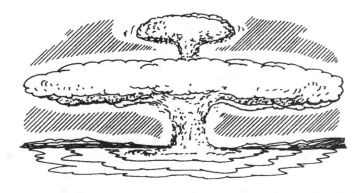

Despite widespread death and destruction, the atomic bomb dropped on Hiroshima on August 6, 1945, did not make the Japanese surrender. President Truman ordered a second bomb to be dropped three days later on Nagasaki. World War II was over.

1. Describe the power of the atomic bomb. _____

    _____

2. Who was Henry Stimson? _____

    _____

3. How did he want to end the war with Japan?_____

    _____

4. How did Japan respond to the warnings of Allied leaders? _____

    _____

5. How did President Truman justify using the A-bomb? _____

    _____

6. Name the two Japanese cities that were bombed to end World War II.

    _____ and _____

7. Do you admire President Truman's ability to make difficult decisions? Do you think Franklin Roosevelt would have decided to bomb Japan if he had been alive? Explain.

    _____

Dwight D. Eisenhower

Presidential Term (1953–1961)

34th

Dwight D. Eisenhower was born October 14, 1890, in Denison, Texas. His father was a mechanic and later the manager of a gas company. His mother was a pacifist. She was deeply saddened at her son's choice of a military career. Eisenhower had five brothers. He grew up in a poor family, wearing hand-me-down clothes and selling produce from his family's garden to make extra money.

He attended public elementary and high schools in Abilene, Kansas. He was an excellent athlete. He attended West Point (1911–1915) where his best subjects were engineering, gunnery, and drill regulation. Eisenhower was a star halfback for the Academy until sidelined by a serious knee injury in 1912. Upon graduation, he was commissioned a second lieutenant and assigned to the Nineteenth Infantry.

Marie "Mamie" Doud married Dwight "Ike" Eisenhower on July 1, 1916. She adjusted easily to military life, moving 28 times before his retirement from the presidency. The couple had one son. As First Lady, mother, and grandmother, Mamie was a very private person. She suffered from Meniere's Disease, an inner-ear disorder, which sometimes made her lose her balance.

Eisenhower was a professional soldier. He served in the Army from 1915–1948 and rose to the rank of five-star general. In December of 1943, President Roosevelt named him supreme allied commander with orders to invade Europe. He planned the successful landing at Normandy, France, on D-Day. Eisenhower resigned from the army in 1948. He was the president of Columbia University (1948–1950) and the supreme commander of the North Atlantic Treaty Organization (1951–1952). He was elected president of the United States in 1952.

In his two terms in office, Eisenhower was a moderate, preferring not to make waves. The Korean War was settled without a winner, and the McCarthy hearings ended. The Civil Rights Act of 1960 prohibited local governments from obstructing the voting rights of black Americans. Federal troops protected black students enrolling at formerly all-white Central High School in Little Rock, Arkansas.

Eisenhower was a popular president. In 1955, a national poll indicated that 60% of Democrats wanted him to be their party's candidate! In 1955, Eisenhower suffered a serious heart attack, but he recovered and was reelected. He was impressed by the concern expressed in thousands of get-well cards and letters. He remained interested in politics during his retirement in Gettysburg, Pennsylvania. Eisenhower died March 28, 1969, of congestive heart failure following surgery.

Suggested Activities/Extensions

1. In 1956, Eisenhower signed a bill authorizing construction of 42,000 miles of interstate highway. Look at a highway map and plot a trip on interstate highways to a popular vacation spot near you. How do your students' families use the highways? How would life be different without them?

2. Alaska and Hawaii were admitted to the Union in 1959. Research important facts about our 49th and 50th states. Locate them on a map. Invite someone who has visited these states to share the experience.

3. Take time to enjoy the entertainment of the "nifty fifties." Play with a hula hoop or Frisbee, read a *Mad* magazine, or listen to an Elvis record.

4. Eisenhower was an excellent cook. One of his favorite foods to prepare was vegetable soup. Share some recipes for vegetable soup and decide on a class favorite.

5. List the characteristics of capitalism and communism. Compare/contrast them. Debate which is the better system. Write dialog for an exchange between Khrushchev and Eisenhower that could have been heard at the "kitchen debate."

6. In 1954, the Supreme Court ruled against racial segregation in public schools. In 1955, Rosa Parks's refusal to give up her seat on the bus for a white person sparked the Montgomery bus boycott. The boycott ended a year later with the Supreme Court decision that segregation on buses was unconstitutional. In 1957 in Little Rock, Arkansas, National Guard troops attempted to block the admission of nine black students to the previously all-white Central High School. The Guard was removed by an order from the Supreme Court, and 1,000 army paratroopers escorted the students to their high school. The fight for civil rights continued throughout this and the next decades.

Rosa Parks

Find out more about this time of racial turmoil and present this information to the class. As a class, compare civil rights issues of the 1950s with those of today. What changes have occurred? Have new issues evolved?

Related Reading

Dwight David Eisenhower, President by Elizabeth Van Steenwyk, Walker, 1987.

Dwight D. Eisenhower by Rafaela Ellis, Garrett, 1989.

Freedom's Children: Young Civil Rights Activists Tell Their Own Stories by Ellen Levine, Putnam, 1993.

Hawaii is a Rainbow by Stephanie Feeney, University of Hawaii Press, 1985.

The Story of Seward's Folly by Susan Clinton, Children's Press, 1987.

Witnesses to Freedom: Young People Who Fought for Civil Rights by Belinda Rochelle, Lodestar, 1993.

Brown v. Board of Education

This case is one of the most important in the history of the Supreme Court. It directly affected segregated schools in twenty-one states and proved that separate schools cannot be truly equal.

There were three cases combined in Brown v. Board of Education.

In the first, Oliver Brown of Topeka, Kansas, sued the Board of Education because his daughter Linda was forced to cross railroad tracks and take a bus to school when a better white school was only five blocks from her home. In the second suit, Briggs v. Clarendon County, twenty black parents sued the Clarendon County, South Carolina, School District because they spent $43 per year on black students and $179 per year on white students. The third case, Davis v. County School Board of Prince Edward County, was filed by the NAACP on behalf of 117 black high school students who were angry about conditions in their school. These three suits were combined when they went before the Supreme Court.

The Supreme Court listened to NAACP lawyer Thurgood Marshall argue for the children, saying that separating people makes them feel inferior. On the other side, John W. Davis argued that the Constitution did not prevent separation and that states had the right to make their own decisions in social matters like segregation. The Court considered the problem for a year. During that time, the chief justice died, and President Eisenhower appointed Earl Warren to take his place.

Earl Warren was able to convince the Supreme Court that the "separate but equal" position had no place in public education.

The Court was unanimous in its decision.

Summarize what you know about Brown v. Board of Education.

The three cases and details:

1. _____
   _____
2. _____
   _____
3. _____
   _____

The two lawyers and their positions:

1. _____
2. _____

The decision: _____

John F. Kennedy

Presidential Term (1961–1963)

35th

John F. Kennedy was born at the family home in Brookline, Massachusetts, on May 29, 1917. He had three sisters and five brothers. His father, Joseph Kennedy, a Harvard graduate, had become a millionaire in the stock market and real estate by age 35. He was ambassador to Great Britain (1937–1940), and opposed the U.S. involvement in World War II. President Kennedy remembered his father as being interested in his children and requiring them to attain high standards.

Kennedy attended Dexter School in Brookline, Massachusetts, Riverdale Country Day School in New York, and Choate Prep School in Wallingford, Connecticut. He was an average student, sometimes more interested in pranks than studying. He majored in political science at Harvard University (1936–1940). He toured Europe after his sophomore year and later worked for his father in Great Britain. He played football and was also on the school's golf and swim teams. A back injury caused him pain throughout his life.

He married Jacqueline Bouvier on September 12, 1953. Mrs. Kennedy had been raised in wealth and was educated at Vassar College (1947–1948) and the Sorbonne in Paris (1949). She had a degree in art from George Washington University (1951) and worked as a photographer for the *Washington Times Herald*. As First Lady, Jackie directed the remodeling of the White House and restoration of the original furnishings. They had one son, John, Jr., and one daughter, Caroline, who were young children during their father's presidency.

John Kennedy served in the navy from 1941–1945. His boat, PT–109, was destroyed and Kennedy heroically led his crew to safety. Following his discharge, Kennedy was U.S. Representative (1947–1953) and U.S. Senator (1953–1961) from Massachusetts. He received the Democratic presidential nomination in 1960. Four televised debates with Richard Nixon were the main focus of the campaign. The youthful, handsome Kennedy was a clear winner over his more experienced opponent.

An important concern during the Kennedy presidency was defeating the communist regime in Cuba. The Bay of Pigs Invasion (1961) was a failure, but President Kennedy ended the Cuban Missile Crisis (1962) with an ultimatum from the U.S. He called for "the prompt dismantling and withdrawal of all offensive weapons from Cuba." The Soviet Union cooperated in exchange for the United States' promise not to invade Cuba. Kennedy ordered an end to discrimination in housing and employment, saying that Americans could not be concerned with freedom around the world if their own land was free to everyone except Negroes.

Kennedy was assassinated in Dallas, Texas, on November 22, 1963. He is buried at Arlington Cemetery. An eternal flame marks his grave.

Suggested Activities/Extensions

1. What is the status of the communist government in Cuba today? Locate Cuba on a map and discuss why/why not we should be concerned about its government. What are the potential problems? What might we do to improve relations between the two countries?

2. The Peace Corps was created in 1961 to provide volunteer services to needy countries. Do you think everyone has an obligation to "give back" to society? Would you consider committing yourself to improving a developing nation? Explain. What can you do to help needy people in your community? Make a list of volunteer opportunities for students.

3. In August 1961, the Berlin Wall was erected to keep Germans in communist East Berlin. The twenty-five-mile wall was built in just four days. President Kennedy made a speech at the Wall, giving hope to Berliners on both sides. Discuss how would you have felt about the Wall as an East Berliner and as a West Berliner. What were your opportunities? problems?

4. Jackie Kennedy was a popular First Lady. She raised two young children in the spotlight of the White House. Read about her feelings on child rearing and share the information with the class.

    How did Jackie's appearance affect fashion trends?

5. John Kennedy was born into a very wealthy family. What would be the best and worst things about such a privileged life? Which would you prefer? Explain. How did Kennedy display his concern for less fortunate people throughout his life?

Jackie Kennedy

Related Reading

Cuba by Clifford W. Crouch, Chelsea House, 1991.

Fantastic Flight to Freedom by Roger Schachtel, Raintree, 1980.

The First Men in Space by Gregory P. Kennedy, Chelsea House, 1991.

Freedom Rides by James Haskins, Hyperion, 1995.

John Fitzgerald Kennedy: America's 35th President by Barry Deneberg, Scholastic, 1988.

The Kennedys by Cass Sendak, Chelsea House, 1991.

The Story of the Peace Corps by Zachary Kent, Children's Press, 1990.

Who Shot the President? The Death of John F. Kennedy by Judy Donnelly, Random House, 1989.

America Enters the Space Race

President Kennedy addressed a joint session of Congress on May 25, 1961, and challenged the United States to land a man on the moon by the end of the decade. The idea excited the American public, and Congress approved funding for the ambitious project. We were in a space race with the Soviet Union.

Three weeks earlier, on May 5, 1961, Alan Shepard became the first American launched into space from Cape Canaveral, Florida. He named his capsule *Freedom 7*. Shepard sat in a fiberglass couch molded to fit his body. The cabin atmosphere was pure oxygen. The launch was delayed two hours and thirty-four minutes because of cloud cover and a computer problem. The Redstone missile that carried the capsule into space performed perfectly. Four minutes and forty-four seconds into the flight, the retro-fire sequence began, and the capsule was in position for reentry. Shepard landed safely in the Atlantic Ocean. The first Project Mercury flight lasted only 15 minutes. Shepard described the experience as "just a pleasant flight." He became an instant national hero.

On February 20, 1962, John Glenn left Cape Canaveral, Florida, and flew three orbits around the Earth. He named his capsule *Friendship 7*. There was trouble near the end of the first orbit and Glenn had to manually control the rest of the flight. NASA was concerned that the capsule might run out of fuel. During the third orbit, mission control told Glenn that his heat shield was loose. It was possible that *Friendship 7* would burn up on reentry. When he reentered the Earth's atmosphere, Glenn lost radio contact with NASA. He saw fire and chunks of burning metal out his window, but suddenly, the parachute opened, and the capsule floated down to the ocean. Later, NASA learned that the loose heat shield signal had been incorrect, but the public praised Glenn as America's first space-age hero.

Choose one of these space flights and use the information to write a news story. Begin with writing statements to answer the following questions:

Who? _____

What? _____

When? _____

Where? _____

Why? _____

How? _____

Write a headline for your article.

_____

_____

_____

Lyndon B. Johnson

Presidential Term (1963–1969)

36th

Lyndon Baines Johnson was born August 27, 1908, in his family's three-room farmhouse in Johnson City, Texas. His father, Sam Johnson, was a teacher and farmer before becoming a member of the Texas House of Representatives. Lyndon had three sisters and one brother. His mother, who was college educated, taught him at home.

By age four, Lyndon was able to read short stories and spell a few easy words. He attended public elementary school and Johnson City High School where he was remembered as being an intelligent but mischievous student. After high school, Lyndon worked odd jobs for two years before agreeing to try college. He attended Southwest Texas State Teachers College (1927–1930) and worked as a teacher before becoming involved in politics. Johnson briefly studied law at Georgetown University (1934–1935).

He was working as personal secretary for Congressman Richard Kleberg when he met Claudia Alta Taylor. They were married November 17, 1934. She was the daughter of a wealthy Texas landowner. As First Lady, she helped win passage of the Highway Beautification Act, restricting billboards and junkyards from major highways. The couple had two daughters, Lynda Bird and Luci Baines. Lynda Bird was married in the White House.

Johnson was the director of the National Youth Administration in Texas (1935–1937) and U.S. Representative from Texas (1937–1949). He was a loyal supporter of Franklin Roosevelt. Johnson won the completion of the Colorado Dam Project for his district. As a U.S. Senator (1949–1960), Johnson became the youngest Democratic majority leader in 1955. He supported an increase in the minimum wage and legislation benefitting the oil and gas interests of Texas. He was Kennedy's choice for vice-presidential running mate and undoubtedly helped him win the South. As vice president, Johnson took a goodwill tour to more than 30 countries.

He assumed the presidency on the death of John Kennedy with a pledge to continue his programs. Johnson's plan for a Great Society included a war on poverty, civil rights laws, Medicare and Medicaid, environmental protection, and several laws to benefit consumers. President Johnson sent the first contingent of Marines to the war in Vietnam. The United States continued to try for a negotiated settlement, but the Vietnamese would not talk until the bombing stopped. The mishandling of the war and failure to reach a settlement were the greatest disappointments of the Johnson presidency.

The Johnsons retired to the LBJ Ranch in Texas January 20, 1969. The former president wrote his memoirs and managed the ranch. He died January 22, 1973, enroute to the hospital after suffering his third heart attack.

Suggested Activities/Extensions

1. Talk with someone who lived during the Vietnam War era. Ask them about the music, fashions, and behavior of antiwar demonstrators. Make banners and buttons with representative slogans. How did nightly television news footage affect their opinions of the war?

2. In February 1964, the Beatles appeared on the Ed Sullivan Show. Soon they had six songs in the Top Ten. Share information and pictures of the Beatles. How are they like or unlike popular musicians today? Listen to several of their songs. Make a list of familiar ones (_Hard Day's Night, I Want to Hold Your Hand_, etc.).

Discuss why the music of the Beatles has lasted for so many years when many other groups fade quickly.

3. Debate the need for a national health care program. Are Medicare and Medicaid enough? If possible, learn about free health care in European countries. How would it change life for your students? their families? private physicians?

4. The Fair Packaging and Labeling Act (1966) required the contents and net quantity be listed on package labels. Do you read labels at the grocery store? How does the information affect what you buy? How does it help people with special dietary requirements? Compare two labels from similar products (like cereals): Which is better for you? Why?

5. The National Traffic Safety Act (1966) required safety standards for all cars beginning with the 1968 model year. Talk with car dealers to learn about safety features in their models.

   Make a list of common features and rate them in order of importance. Graph how many of your classmates use seat belts all the time, some of the time, or never.

6. Martin Luther King, Jr., was assassinated on April 4, 1968, in Memphis, Tennessee. He had lived a life of nonviolence. How did his loss change the civil rights movement? How have his followers (including his wife) continued his dream?

Related Reading

The Department of Health and Human Services by Merle Broberg, Chelsea House, 1989.

Lyndon B. Johnson by Jim Hargrove, Children's Press, 1987.

Martin Luther King by Rosemary L. Bray, Greenwillow, 1995.

War in Vietnam (a four-volume set) by David K. Wright, Children's Press, 1989.

The Great Society

As president, Johnson was concerned about Americans living in poverty. He hoped to create a "Great Society," attacking discrimination, poverty, and environmental problems. Many of these domestic programs were a great success; however, they were expensive. Conservatives felt that the country could not afford the "war on poverty" while fighting the war in Vietnam. Here are some of the laws and programs enacted by Congress for the "Great Society":

- **Civil Rights Act (1964)**–prohibited discrimination in the use of federal funds and ended segregation in public places and employment.

- **Headstart**–helped preschoolers prepare for kindergarten.

- **Job Corps**–trained people who were unemployed.

- **Neighborhood Youth Corps**–found work for needy teenagers.

- **Elementary and Secondary Education Ac**t–increased federal aid to schools.

- **Medicaid**–provided medical care for poor people.

- **Medicare**–paid hospital bills for elderly people.

- **Air Quality Act (1967)**–assisted states in setting and enforcing air quality standards.

- **Water Quality Act (1965)**–established water quality standards.

Assignment: Choose one of the laws from the above list. Complete the chart, explaining how it affects you and your family, your community, state, and the country.

Law:			
Effects on . . .			
Me and My Family	**My Community**	**My State**	**My Country**

Richard M. Nixon

Presidential Term (1969–1974)

37th

Richard Milhous Nixon was born January 9, 1913, at his family's home in Yorba Linda, California. Milhous was his mother's maiden name. He was the second of five sons born into the Quaker family. His father, Francis Anthony Nixon, became a Republican the day President William McKinley passed through his hometown and complimented him on his fine horse. Nixon's mother, Hannah, was a devoutly religious woman who wanted Richard to become a Quaker missionary.

Richard attended public elementary and high schools in Yorba Linda and Whittier, California. He was first in his high school graduating class and was voted best all-around student. He graduated from Whittier College (1934) and Duke University Law School (1937). Nixon was admitted to the California bar in 1937.

Richard and Thelma "Pat" Nixon were married on June 21, 1940, in Riverside, California. She was orphaned at 17 and worked odd jobs in New York and California. She earned money as an extra in films. Pat was graduated from the University of Southern California (1937). She was a very private First Lady. The Nixons had two daughters, Patricia, who was married at the White House, and Julie, who married the grandson of former President Eisenhower.

Richard Nixon rejected the Quaker teachings of pacificism and joined the navy during World War II. He was cited for meritorious performance in the South Pacific. In 1946, he upset the incumbent U.S. Representative from California's Twelfth Congressional District (1947–1950). He was a U.S. Senator (1951–1953) and vice president under Dwight Eisenhower (1953–1961). Nixon was defeated in the 1960 presidential election by John Kennedy. From 1963–1968 he practiced law in New York. He campaigned for Republican Barry Goldwater in 1964. Richard M. Nixon was elected president in 1968 and again in 1972.

He reduced the U.S. involvement in Vietnam but expanded the fighting into Laos and Cambodia. In August 1972, the last troops were withdrawn. In February 1972, Nixon became the first president to make a "journey for peace" to China. The two governments agreed to broaden trade, scientific, and cultural contacts. The Environmental Protection Agency was formed in 1970 to regulate, reduce, and control pollution. On June 17, 1972, five agents were arrested breaking into the Democratic National Headquarters in Washington, D.C. The "Watergate Incident" became the worst political scandal in American history. The House Judiciary Committee approved three articles of impeachment against the president. Richard Nixon was forced to resign in disgrace.

In his resignation address to the people, Nixon only admitted errors in judgement. He and Mrs. Nixon retired to their home in San Clemente, California. He was pardoned of all federal crimes by his successor, President Gerald Ford. Richard Nixon died on April 22, 1994, after suffering a stroke.

Suggested Activities/Extensions

1. On July 20, 1969, Neil Armstrong and Edwin Aldrin landed on the moon. The astronauts, including Michael Collins, the pilot of the command ship, were able to talk with President Nixon from outer space. Interview someone who remembers the televised landing. Ask that person to recount the experience. Read more to determine the value of space exploration to society. What plans does NASA currently have for more exploration? Use your imagination to brainstorm interesting possibilities for future space travel.

Neil Armstrong

2. The Environmental Protection Agency was created by executive order of President Nixon on December 2, 1970. Its function is to establish and enforce national standards for air and water quality. President Nixon was committed to protecting the environment. Choose a project for your class or school to adopt as a way to improve the environment. It may be something like recycling used copy paper or asking your cafeteria to stop using disposable plastic utensils and containers. Make posters and plan a rally to gain support for your cause.

3. The first Earth Day was organized on April 22, 1970. It was intended to focus public attention on environmental issues of land, air, and water pollution. What can you do to celebrate Earth Day?

   Make a chart divided into three sections: land, water, air. List environmental problems and possible solutions.

4. The women's liberation movement was an outgrowth of the civil rights movement and antiwar protests. Women were determined to be treated as equals to men under the law. Research the work of early activists like Betty Friedan and discuss the changes that occurred in women's roles during the 50s and 60s. Compare/contrast problems of discrimination against women and blacks.

Related Reading

The Environmental Protection Agency by Kevin J. Law, Chelsea House, 1988.

One Giant Leap by Mary Ann Fraser, Holt, 1993.

Richard M. Nixon by Jim Hargrave, Children's Press, 1985.

Save the Earth by Betty Miles, Knopf, 1991.

War in Vietnam (a four-volume set) by David K. Wright, Children's Press, 1989.

The Story of Watergate

On June 17, 1972, five men were arrested burglarizing the Democratic National Headquarters of the Watergate Hotel in Washington, D.C. They were planting listening devices. They worked for the Committee to Re-elect President Nixon. The White House tried to ignore the charges, but it became the worst political scandal in American history and forced the resignation of President Richard Nixon.

Two reporters for the *Washington Post,* Bob Woodward and Carl Bernstein, uncovered a series of misdeeds done by people working for Nixon. In addition to planting the listening devices, Nixon's people tried to cover up their crime with hush money and stole confidential papers about the Vietnam War. They tapped telephone lines of people Nixon disliked. The Nixon administration was determined to use the power of the government to bring down their political enemies.

President Nixon denied authorizing the Watergate break-in, but John Dean, a White House attorney, proved that he had directed the cover-up that followed. The truth was told on tapes of White House phone conversations that Richard Nixon kept to help in the future writing of his memoirs. The Supreme Court ordered Nixon to turn over the tapes for the investigation. Special prosecutors, Archibald Cox and Leon Jaworski, convicted several of the president's aides. They were sentenced to prison.

Three articles of impeachment were approved against Richard Nixon for obstruction of justice, abuse of power, and failure to comply with congressional subpoenas. The president resigned on August 9, 1974, to avoid impeachment proceedings. President Ford pardoned Nixon of all wrongdoing shortly after assuming office.

Use the information in the above paragraphs to fill in the blanks below.

Problem _____

Reporters _____ and _____

Crimes _____ , _____

_____ , _____

Prosecutors _____ and _____

Results for Nixon aides _____

Articles of Impeachment _____ ,

_____ and _____

Result for Nixon _____

Discuss: Do you think that President Ford made the right decision in pardoning Nixon? What effect would the impeachment proceedings have had on the country? Nixon? the Ford administration?

Gerald R. Ford

Presidential Term (1974–1977)

38th

Gerald Ford was born Leslie Lynch King, Jr., on July 14, 1913, in Omaha, Nebraska. He was named after his biological father, whom he only met twice. His biological parents were divorced when Ford was an infant. His mother moved with her son to her parents' home in Grand Rapids where she met and married Gerald Rudolf Ford. He adopted her son, who was renamed Gerald Rudolf Ford, Jr. The senior Ford owned a paint store in Grand Rapids, Michigan.

Ford attended public elementary and high schools in Grand Rapids where he excelled in history and government. He was the star center for the high school football team. He won a partial scholarship to the University of Michigan to study economics and political science. He was named the most valuable player in the 1935 College All-Star game against the Chicago Bears. He turned down professional football contracts from the Detroit Lions and the Green Bay Packers in order to attend law school. He was admitted to the Michigan bar in June 1941.

He married Elizabeth Ann Bloomer on October 15, 1948. They had grown up together in Grand Rapids but went different ways as young adults. Betty was divorced and had been working as a dancer and model in New York. As First Lady, she spoke out in favor of abortion, the Equal Rights Amendment, and the appointment of a woman to the Supreme Court. She established the Betty Ford Clinic, a chemical dependency recovery center because of her own problems with prescription drugs and alcohol. The Fords have four children: three sons and one daughter.

Gerald Ford was elected twelve times to the U.S. House of Representatives (1949–1973) and was the minority leader (1965–1973). He was a moderate conservative and personal friend of Richard Nixon. Following Vice President Spiro T. Agnew's resignation in October of 1973, Ford was appointed to that position. He took the oath of office on December 6, 1973, and later became president of the United States on the resignation of Richard Nixon August 9, 1974. Gerald Ford was the first man in history to become both vice president and president without having been elected to either office.

The new president appointed Nelson A. Rockefeller vice president in December 1974. Ford was an energetic and enthusiastic leader, particularly interested in continuing the foreign policies of his predecessor. One month after taking office, President Ford pardoned Richard Nixon of all crimes that he may have committed while president. He survived two assassination attempts in September 1975.

After his reelection defeat, the Fords retired to Rancho Mirage, California. Mr. and Mrs. Ford have both written their memoirs. President Ford maintains a busy schedule as a public speaker.

Suggested Activities/Extensions

1. As president, Ford traveled to Japan, the Soviet Union, West Germany, Poland, Finland, France, and China in an effort to improve foreign relations, particularly with communist bloc nations. Locate these countries on a map of the world and discuss how their governments have changed since the 70s.

2. In 1973, Arab nations imposed an oil embargo on the United States. Within a year, gasoline prices increased 70%. Ask your parents about the consequences of the oil embargo. What can your family do to limit gasoline consumption? Check the price per gallon at your local station. Allowing for a 70% increase, how much did the gas cost per gallon in 1973? Talk about how to calculate the cost per mile of running your family car, using current gasoline prices.

3. Discuss the pros and cons of Ford's decision to pardon Richard Nixon. Make a graph showing what the members of your class would have done in Ford's place.

4. In his inaugural address, President Ford said, "I believe that truth is the glue that holds government together, not only our government but civilization itself .... As we bind up the wounds of Watergate ... let us restore the golden rule to our political process ...." How important do you believe it is to be truthful? Explain. How would your life be improved if everyone behaved according to the golden rule (do unto others as you would have others do unto you)? Apply these concepts to real-life situations.

5. First Lady Betty Ford is most remembered for her candor regarding her personal life. When she spoke publicly about her battle with breast cancer, she raised public awareness of the disease and served as an inspiration to others who faced cancer. As First Lady, Betty Ford also supported the Equal Rights Amendment and valued both the traditional role of women and the role of women in the workplace. After leaving the White House, Mrs. Ford publicly described her struggle with addiction to alcohol and pain medication, and she founded the Betty Ford Clinic for substance abuse in Rancho Mirage, California. Find out more about this remarkable First Lady and report your findings to the class.

Betty Ford

Extension: As a class project, research the first ladies and present short biographies of each in a class book. Include pictures of each. Where possible, compare the lives and achievements of some of the first ladies.

Related Reading

Gerald R. Ford by David R. Collins, Garrett, 1990.

Gerald R. Ford President by Sallie G. Randolph, Walker, 1987.

War in Vietnam (a four-volume set) by David K. Wright, Children's Press, 1989.

The Nation's Bicentennial

Gerald Ford was president during the country's bicentennial celebration. Pretend that you could go back in time to 1976. What would you do to celebrate the 200th birthday of America?

Choose a project to do with a group of your friends.

Here are some ideas:

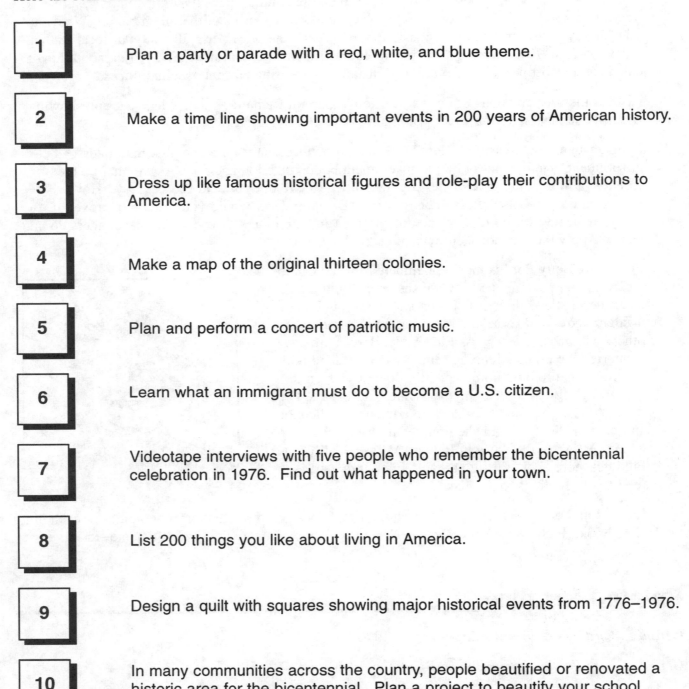

1 Plan a party or parade with a red, white, and blue theme.

2 Make a time line showing important events in 200 years of American history.

3 Dress up like famous historical figures and role-play their contributions to America.

4 Make a map of the original thirteen colonies.

5 Plan and perform a concert of patriotic music.

6 Learn what an immigrant must do to become a U.S. citizen.

7 Videotape interviews with five people who remember the bicentennial celebration in 1976. Find out what happened in your town.

8 List 200 things you like about living in America.

9 Design a quilt with squares showing major historical events from 1776–1976.

10 In many communities across the country, people beautified or renovated a historic area for the bicentennial. Plan a project to beautify your school grounds or community.

Jimmy Carter

Presidential Term (1977–1981)

39th

James Earl Carter, Jr., was born October 1, 1924, in Wise Hospital in Plains, Georgia. He is the first president to have been born in a hospital. Jimmy had two sisters and one brother. When he was four years old, the Carter family moved to Archery, Georgia, a mostly black community. They had no running water or electricity in their home, so entertainment was limited to reading or listening to a battery operated radio. He worked in the fields, and at age five remembers selling boiled peanuts in the streets of Plains, Georgia. Carter attended elementary and high schools in Plains. He is remembered as an intelligent, well-behaved student. His best subjects were literature and history. Carter was admitted to the Naval Academy at Annapolis in 1943. His best subjects were gunnery, naval tactics, and electronics. Upon graduation he intended to become a career naval officer.

James Earl Carter, Jr., and Eleanor Rosalynn Smith were married July 7, 1946, at the Plains, Georgia, Methodist Church. Rosalynn had been a childhood friend of Jimmy's sister, Ruth, who introduced the couple. She had been valedictorian of her high school class and attended Georgia Southwestern College for two years. As First Lady, Mrs. Carter testified before Congress on behalf of mental health programs and the Equal Rights Amendment. The Carters have four children, three sons and a daughter, Amy, who was nine years old when her father was elected president.

Jimmy Carter served in the navy from 1946–1953. He was chosen by Admiral Hyman Rickover to be engineering officer of the *Sea Wolf*, one of the first atomic submarines. He resigned from the navy when his father died to return to Plains, Georgia, and manage the family peanut business. In Plains he was active in civic affairs and called for racial tolerance after the Brown v. Board of Education decision (p.116). Carter was governor of Georgia (1971–1975), interested in issues of racial discrimination, mental health, and the environment. He was popular with common people because of his casual manner and genuine smile.

Carter's greatest achievement as president was at Camp David in 1978, when a peace agreement was signed, ending a 31-year state of war between Israel and Egypt. On November 4, 1979, Iranian militants stormed the U.S. embassy and took several Americans hostage. Carter did not give in to terrorism, and 52 Americans were held for 444 days. There was one failed rescue attempt. This incident led to his defeat in the 1980 election.

In retirement, Carter is busy working for Habitat for Humanity, a nonprofit organization that builds low-cost housing, lecturing in political science at Emory University, and mediating human rights and peace agreements around the world.

Suggested Activities/Extensions

1. James Earl Carter, Sr., ran a profitable peanut business in Plains, Georgia. Jimmy continued the family business after his father's death in 1953. Read more about the work of George Washington Carver who, in his laboratory at Tuskegee Institute, developed over a hundred uses for the peanut. Have students share recipes and foods made from peanuts.

2. Make some peanut butter. You will need about a cup (250 mL) of shelled peanuts, a food processor, and 2 tablespoons (30 mL) of vegetable oil. Remove the red skins from the peanuts and process to the desired consistency, adding the oil a little at a time. You may wish to add a little salt. Serve on crackers or bread.

3. If you wish, plant some raw, unshelled peanuts. Simply crack the shell open and plant the whole thing about two inches deep in a pot of loose, sandy soil. Keep them watered. Your peanuts should sprout in about two weeks.

4. In 1979, the Organization of Petroleum Exporting Countries (OPEC) doubled the price for a barrel of oil. This led to a shortage of affordable gasoline. People began to buy fuel efficient imported cars, and American automobile manufacturers laid off workers. Brainstorm a list of ways people can avoid using their automobiles. Discuss alternative fuels (electric or solar powered cars) as a way to reduce our dependency on foreign oil.

5. In March 1979, an accident took place at the nuclear power plant at Three-Mile Island near Harrisburg, Pennsylvania. This touched off a series of demonstrations around the country by protestors trying to stop the building of more nuclear facilities. Discuss the pros and cons of nuclear energy, along with its importance in light of the energy crisis.

6. During Jimmy Carter's presidency, many events unfolded which would have an impact on the United States and the world. Among these events are the following:
   - Violence sweeps Nicaragua as Sandanista guerrillas attempt to overthrow the government.
   - In England, the first test-tube baby is born.
   - More than 900 Americans commit suicide in Jim Jones' People's Temple in Guyana, South America.
   - Earthquakes hit Greece, Japan, Mexico, Iran, and central Europe.
   - John Paul II becomes the first Polish pope.
   - A massive oil spill occurs along the coast of France when the tanker *Amoco Cadiz* wrecks.
   - The Camp David Accord leads to an Egypt-Israel peace treaty.
   - Mother Teresa wins the Nobel Peace Prize.
   - Russia invades Afghanistan.
   - The United States and China establish diplomatic relations.

Expand this list of events and create a classroom time line (1977–1981) to display on a wall. As an extension, make similar time lines for the remaining presidents in this unit.

Related Reading

The Arab-Israeli Conflict by Paul J. Deegan, Abdo and Daughters, 1991.

Jimmy Carter by Betsy Covington Smith, Walker, 1986.

Jimmy Carter by Ed Slavin, Chelsea, 1989.

A Pocketful of Goobers: A Story About George Washington Carver by Barbara Mitchell, Carolrhoda, 1986.

The Camp David Accords

President Carter is recognized for his ability as a negotiator. He is able to understand both sides of a disagreement and suggest a compromise that is acceptable to everyone.

He invited Egyptian President Anwar Sadat and Israeli Prime Minister Menachem Begin to the presidential retreat at Camp David, Maryland, in September 1978. The three leaders participated in 13 days of private negotiations in an effort to bring peace to the Middle East.

On September 17, President Carter was able to announce that a workable compromise had been reached. Further negotiations would be necessary, but significant progress had been made. A document called a Framework for Peace in the Middle East was signed before television cameras.

On March 26, 1979, Begin and Sadat signed a treaty called the Camp David Accords, which ended the 31-year state of war between their two countries.

Assignment: Suppose you were a speech writer for President Carter. Write a brief statement for him to give the press at the signing of the peace treaty. Include information about the time and place, parties and countries involved, the problem that was solved, and how the world will benefit from the decision.

My Fellow Americans:

Ronald Reagan

Presidential Term (1981–1989)

40th

Ronald Wilson Reagan was born February 6, 1911, at his parents' apartment in Tampico, Illinois. His family moved to several small towns in Illinois during Ron's childhood. His father was a store manager. With his older brother Neil, Ron (nicknamed "Dutch" at birth by his father) enjoyed exploring the countryside and swimming in the summer and sledding and skating in the winter.

His mother taught him to read before he entered elementary school. He was a good student in high school and a star athlete, playing on the football, basketball, and track teams. As a senior, he was student body president and appeared in school plays. Those experiences helped interest Ron in becoming an actor. He continued his education at Eureka College (1928–1932), majoring in sociology and economics. He was active in student government and on the football, track, and swim teams. Reagan received honors for his performance in a play, *Aria da Capo* by Edna St.Vincent Millay. Upon graduation, he decided to accept a job as a sports announcer at a small radio station in Davenport, Iowa.

He married actress Jane Wyman on January 26, 1940. The couple had one daughter, Maureen (1941), and adopted a son, Michael, in 1945. The marriage suffered because of work pressures and differing political views. They were divorced on June 28, 1948. Four years later, Reagan married Nancy Davis on March 4, 1952. She supported him through his political campaigns. As First Lady, she initiated the "Just Say No" program to attack the problem of drugs and alcohol in America. The Reagans have two children, a son and a daughter.

After serving in the army reserve during World War II, Ronald Reagan was determined to enter show business. He was a successful actor for Warner Brothers Studio and television host of the *General Electric Theater* and *Death Valley Days* before entering politics. He served as governor of California from 1968–1975, restricting the size and cost of state government, increasing the income tax, and imposing new requirements on welfare eligibility. Because he was a popular and effective governor, Reagan received the Republican nomination for president in 1980. As president, Reagan was able to slow inflation and create new jobs. He survived an assassination attempt in 1981. His administration regularly opposed acts of terrorism around the world. The most serious controversy of his presidency involved the sale of arms to Iran and the channeling of profits to the Nicaraguan Contras. Relations with the Soviet Union improved in 1985 under President Mikhail Gorbachev. The two leaders signed the Intermediate-range Nuclear Forces Treaty in 1987. Both countries agreed to destroy hundreds of medium- and short-range missiles.

On January 20, 1989, the Reagans retired to their home in Bel Air, California. The former president is currently being treated for Alzheimer's Disease.

Suggested Activities/Extensions

1. Ronald Reagan was an actor before entering politics. His first lasting performance was in *Knute Rockne—All American* (1940). If possible, arrange a showing of the former president in his role as the "Gipper." Discuss the personal characteristics that made Reagan a popular actor and politician.

2. Reagan acted against terrorism around the world, particularly the countries of Iran, Libya, North Korea, Cuba, and Nicaragua. Research the administration's response to terrorist acts in these countries and locate them on a map. Do you believe the United States should ever negotiate with terrorists? Explain.

3. The *Challenger* space shuttle exploded on January 28, 1986. It was the first time Americans had lost their lives in the space program. Talk with someone who remembers the incident to learn how it shocked the nation. Make a list of words that describe their feelings. Write a sentence for each word.

4. Nancy Reagan began the "Just Say No" campaign in response to drug and alcohol abuse among school children. Is there a "Just Say No" club at your school? Is it effective? How do students in your school learn about substance abuse? Work in groups to list ten problems that result from substance abuse. Combine all the lists during a class discussion.

Sandra Day O' Connor

5. President Reagan appointed the first woman, Sandra Day O'Connor, to the Supreme Court. Read more about her and write a short report to share with the class. Explain the process for being appointed and confirmed a Supreme Court justice.

6. Ronald Reagan began eating jelly beans after he stopped smoking. Bring in three to four pounds of jelly beans to sort and graph by color, and then divide them among class members for a snack. Make a list showing favorite flavors in descending order.

Related Reading

Good Answers to Tough Questions About Substance Abuse by Joy Berry, Children's Press, 1990.

The Picture Life of Ronald Reagan by Don Lawson, Watts, 1985.

Ronald Reagan by George Sullivan, Messner, 1985.

Space Shuttle Challenger: Explosion by Sue L. Hamilton, Abdo and Daughters, 1988.

Star Wars by Christopher Lampton, Watts, 1987.

Budget

When Ronald Reagan took office, the country already had a big debt (deficit). Income taxes were not enough to pay the bills, so the deficit grew at an unbelievable rate, from $58 billion in 1981 (when Reagan took office) to $2.3 trillion in 1988 (when he left office). The interest on the national debt was $150 billion a year.

Assignment: In 1981, Reagan proposed a plan that would cut taxes, reduce welfare, unemployment, and other programs, and increase the defense budget. His economis policies became known as "*Reaganomics*." Use the space below to design a political cartoon depicting one of the aspects of Reaganomics.

Political Cartoon

What Does This Mean to You?

When you spend more than you earn, you have to borrow money to pay your bills. You go into debt. Then you must pay interest on the borrowed money, which makes repaying the loan more difficult. Suppose you have an allowance of $_____ per week. You need to budget that amount to pay for clothing, entertainment, fast food, and savings. How would you spend your money?

Clothing _____   Fast Food _____

Entertainment _____   Savings _____

What lessons about managing money can you learn from this?

_____

_____

_____

George Bush

Presidential Term (1989–1993)

41st

George Herbert Walker Bush was born June 12, 1924, in the family home in Milton, Massachusetts. There were five children in the Bush family. George's father, Prescott Bush, was a Wall Street banker and member of the Connecticut senate. His mother, Dorothy, was a strong disciplinarian. She did not want her children to be spoiled by the wealth around them.

Bush attended the Greenwich Connecticut Country Day School and Phillips Academy, where he was a good student and versatile athlete, playing on the football, soccer, and tennis teams. He enlisted in the navy before going to college. After the war, George married and enrolled in an accelerated program at Yale University. He majored in economics and graduated with honors in 1948.

George Bush and Barbara Pierce were married January 6, 1945 in Rye, New York. They were introduced through a mutual friend, Jack Wozencraft, and both agreed it was "love at first sight." The Bush's have four sons and one daughter. As First Lady, Mrs. Bush actively promoted adult literacy and children's programs like Head Start and Chapter One Reading.

George enlisted in the navy on his eighteenth birthday. He flew 58 combat missions in the Pacific and was one of only four pilots in his squadron to survive the war. Upon graduation from Yale, the Bushes moved to Texas. While there, George Bush worked in the oil business from 1948–1966. He became active in Republican politics and was elected U.S. Representative from Texas (1967–1971). Following that, President Nixon appointed him U.S. Ambassador to the United Nations (1971–1973). Bush hoped to become vice president under Gerald Ford, but he was not chosen. Ford offered him an ambassadorship instead, and Bush selected China, where he remained for 13 months. He was the director of the Central Intelligence Agency (1976–1977) and vice president of the United States under Ronald Reagan (1981–1989).

As president, George Bush acknowledged the national deficit to be his greatest concern. He had pledged no new taxes during his campaign, but he later agreed to a series of tax hikes on gasoline, cigarettes, beer, luxury items, and the top income tax rates. In 1989, the president signed into law a plan to bail out failed savings and loans. American forces invaded Panama to capture Manuel Noriega who was wanted in Florida on drug trafficking charges. In November 1990, Bush met with Mikhail Gorbachev and leaders from twenty other NATO countries to sign a treaty ending the Cold War. The Soviet Union agreed to a phased withdrawal from all its satellites in Eastern Europe. The United States sent troops to the Persian Gulf (1990) when Iraq invaded Kuwait.

George and Barbara Bush retired to Houston, Texas, after the inauguration of Bill Clinton in 1992.

Suggested Activities/Extensions

1. President Bush said publicly that he did not like broccoli. Research the nutritional value of the vegetable and gather a group of recipes that might make it more palatable. Graph your students' opinions of broccoli. If appropriate, enjoy a broccoli buffet!

2. Bush pledged to be the "environmental president." He participated in the United Nations Earth Summit held in Rio De Janeiro, Brazil, on June 14, 1992. Along with leaders from 153 nations, he signed a pledge to address environmental problems. Choose one of these to research and report on:

   - greenhouse effect
   - destruction of the rain forest
   - urban smog
   - oil spills (*Exxon Valdez*)
   - depletion of the ozone

3. Mrs. Bush founded an organization for adult literacy. How would your life be different if you could not read? Consider volunteering some time to help a child (or adult) practice reading. Make a pledge to use your public library.

4. Read more about Nelson Mandela and apartheid in South Africa. The African National Congress leader was released from prison in February 1990 so that he could negotiate a peaceful end to apartheid with President F. W. deKlerk. How is Nelson Mandela similar to Dr. Martin Luther King, Jr.? What characteristics make him an effective leader?

5. The Americans with Disabilities Act of 1990 required that all businesses, public buildings, and transportation be made accessible to wheelchairs. Make a list of changes that have taken place in your community since the passage of that law.

6. The United States launched Operation Desert Storm on January 17, 1991. It was a short, powerful war, ending on February 27.

   The victory boosted President Bush's approval rating to 89%, the highest ever recorded in a Gallup Poll. Assign your class to poll 100 people regarding their opinion of the current president. Report back to the group. What is his approval rating?

7. George Bush encouraged volunteerism in the country with his "thousand points of light" program. Discuss volunteer opportunities available for teenagers in your community. If appropriate, adopt a class project. How important are volunteers?

Related Reading _____

Barbara Bush: First Lady of Literacy by June Behrens, Children's Press, 1990.

George Bush: The Story of the Forty-first President of the United States by Mark Sufrin, Dell, 1989.

Nelson Mandela by Brian Feinberg, Chelsea Juniors, 1992.

The Picture Life of George Bush by Ron Schneiderman, Watts, 1989.

The U. S. Navy by Kathy Pelta, Lerner, 1990.

The Collapse of Communism

In 1989, the Union of Soviet Socialist Republics fell apart. Communism had failed as a political and economic system. The overthrow of communism marked the end of the Cold War and a change in world politics. Under Mikhail Gorbachev, the Soviet Union stopped trying to force communism on other countries; so, one by one the countries rejected Marxism and adopted some form of democracy. Here is what happened:

Mikhail Gorbachev

- In December of 1990, Poland elected Lech Walesa president of the first noncommunist government since World War II.

- The border of East and West Germany was opened to free travel on November 9, 1989.

- Romania, Hungary, Bulgaria, and Albania ousted their communist leaders and moved toward free elections and a democratic way of life.

- The former Soviet Union broke into the Baltic Republics, Russia, Ukraine, and Byelorussia. President Gorbachev resigned on Christmas Day 1991.

When George Bush left office, the only remaining communist countries were Cuba, North Korea, and China.

How do you think the collapse of communism affects the United States in these areas?

- space program _____

- export business _____

- defense spending _____

- immigration laws _____

- foreign aid _____

What effect would the collapse have on the remaining communist countries?

_____

_____

_____

_____

_____

Bill Clinton

Presidential Term (1993-)

42nd

William Jefferson Blythe IV was born August 19, 1946, at Julia Chester Hospital in Hope, Arkansas. His father, William Jefferson Blythe III was a traveling salesman killed in an automobile accident before his son's birth. His stepfather, Roger Clinton (who adopted him), was an abusive alcoholic who died of cancer in 1968. Clinton's mother was a nurse. He has one half brother, Roger. As a young child, Bill lived with his grandparents while his mother studied nursing in New Orleans. They taught him to read and count by age three and impressed him with their belief in racial tolerance while living in the segregated South. When Clinton was seven years old, he moved with his family to Hot Springs, Arkansas, where he attended public schools. He enjoyed playing saxophone in the school band and was offered a scholarship to study music. Bill decided to attend Georgetown University because of his interest in politics and foreign service. He graduated with a degree in international affairs in 1968. The following fall, Clinton moved to England to study at Oxford University as a Rhodes scholar. After two years, he accepted a scholarship to Yale University, where he received his law degree in 1973.

Hillary Rodham and Bill Clinton met in the Yale University law library and were married on October 11, 1975. They have one daughter, Chelsea. While still a law student, Mrs. Clinton worked with the Children's Defense Fund. In 1974, she was one of the lawyers for the House Judiciary Committee considering impeachment charges against President Richard Nixon. As First Lady, Hillary headed the Task Force on National Health Care Reform.

Bill Clinton was professor of law at the University of Arkansas (1973–1976) before becoming attorney general of Arkansas (1977–1979). In 1978, he was named one of the Ten Outstanding Young Men in the country by the Junior Chamber of Commerce. At age 32, Clinton became the youngest governor in the country, serving Arkansas from 1979–1981 and 1983–1992. He brought many new jobs to Arkansas, worked for improved health care, and supported education reform. He resigned the governorship to run for president of the United States.

In his presidential campaign, Clinton proposed a tax hike on the richest 2% of Americans with modest tax cuts for the middle class. He supported public works projects (like the New Deal, p.107) to build a high speed rail service and rebuild the nation's highways. He proposed a national health care program with affordable coverage for all and welfare reform that would require recipients to return to work in two years or lose their benefits.

On election night, the Clinton-Gore era began with "high hopes and brave hearts." To their supporters, they offered a fresh start for America.

Suggested Activities/Extensions

1. President Clinton plays the saxophone. Read about the invention of this instrument in an encyclopedia or music dictionary. If possible, invite someone to bring a saxophone to your class so that students may see and hear the instrument.

2. Bill Clinton was the governor of Arkansas for longer than anyone except Orval E. Faubus and the only governor to have been reelected after defeat. Make a list of other presidents who have served as governors.

3. Hillary Clinton was appointed by her husband to head a task force on health care reform. Some people want to end the high costs and insurance red tape in our health care system. Others believe that our health care system does not need changing. What do you think would be a perfect health care plan for America? What problems stand in the way of health care reform?

4. Chelsea Clinton attends a private school in Washington, D.C. She attended public schools when her father was governor of Arkansas. What similarities and differences do you think Chelsea has noticed about the schools she has attended? Has anyone in your class attended both types of schools?

5. Learn more about President Clinton's home state of Arkansas.

   Prepare a list of questions about the history, people, land, and economy that can be answered from books (below) or an encyclopedia. Pass your questions to a friend to answer.

6. The Brady Bill became law on November 30, 1993. It imposes a five-day waiting period and background search before a person may buy a hand gun. There is also a ban on nineteen types of assault weapons. Do you think these bills are helpful? Debate the pros and cons of gun ownership. The Crime Bill (September 13, 1994) attacks crime by adding 100,000 police officers, funding prevention programs, and building prisons. Try to find out if your community has benefitted from the Crime Bill. What do you think can be done to prevent children from committing crimes?

7. The Clinton administration won passage of the North American Free Trade Agreement (NAFTA) December 8, 1993. Trade barriers will be eliminated between the United States and Canada and Mexico. This law lowered import taxes and the cost of goods from Canada and Mexico. Learn more about Canada and Mexico and make a list of exports from each country.

Related Reading

Arkansas by Ann Heinrichs, Children's Press, 1989.

Bill Clinton by Robert Cwiklik, Millbrook Press, 1993.

Hillary Rodham Clinton by JoAnn Bren Guernsey, Lerner, 1993.

William Jefferson Clinton by Zachary Kent, Children's Press, 1993.

Issues

There are many serious problems in the United States today. It is the president's job to support laws and programs that improve the American way of life. Here are some of the issues President Clinton's administration is facing:

- gun control
- education reform
- increased taxes
- welfare reform

- budget deficit reduction
- health care reform
- drug/alcohol abuse

- creating new jobs
- teenage pregnancy
- violent crime rate

List these issues in order of importance to your future.

1. _____
2. _____
3. _____
4. _____
5. _____
6. _____
7. _____
8. _____
9. _____
10. _____

If you were president, what actions would you take to address and resolve the first issue?

What other problems should be added to this list?

_____

_____

_____

_____

_____

Fascinating Presidential Facts

- Five presidents died during their first terms in office: William Henry Harrison, Zachary Taylor, James Garfield, Warren Harding, and John Kennedy.

- The only president to keep his original cabinet for four years was Franklin Pierce.

- These presidents kept unusual pets:

    John Quincy Adams raised silkworms.
    Thomas Jefferson had a pet mockingbird.
    Theodore Roosevelt had a young lion and several bear cubs.
    Andrew Johnson kept white mice.
    William Howard Taft allowed a cow to graze the lawn.
    William McKinley had a parrot and some roosters.
    Zachary Taylor's horse, Whitey, roamed the White House lawn.

- Two dogs, Liberty (a golden retriever owned by the Fords) and Millie (a springer spaniel owned by the Bushes), gave birth to puppies while at the White House.

- Franklin Roosevelt liked to eat fish for breakfast.

- Grover Cleveland once said that he preferred pickled herring, cheese, and a chop to the fancy food served at the White House.

- Amy Carter was the first presidential child to attend public school since Theodore Roosevelt's time.

- The Baby Ruth candy bar was named after the daughter of Grover Cleveland, the first baby born in the White House.

- Harry Truman was the only modern (20th century) president who did not attend college.

- William Howard Taft, who weighed more than 300 pounds, got stuck in the White House bathtub.

- George Washington's mother once wrote to government leaders, complaining that she needed money because George was not taking care of her.

- John Quincy Adams used to get up two hours before sunrise to go skinny dipping in the Potomac River.

- Andrew Jackson had a bullet in his chest from fighting a duel over his wife's honor. The bullet could not be removed because it was too close to his heart.

- An 11-year-old girl advised Abraham Lincoln to grow a beard.

- Andrew Johnson, a tailor, made a lot of his own clothes.

- Benjamin Harrison was so afraid of the electric lights in the White House he asked the servants to turn them on and off.

- Theodore Roosevelt once boxed John Sullivan, the heavyweight champion of the world, in the White House gym.

- Woodrow Wilson had a small flock of sheep "mow" the lawn during World War I. Mrs. Wilson sold the wool from the sheep and gave the money to the Red Cross.

- Franklin D. Roosevelt's favorite hobby was stamp collecting.

- President Lyndon Johnson gave his friends toothbrushes so they would think of him first thing in the morning and last thing at night.

- President Gerald Ford was featured on the cover of *Cosmopolitan* magazine dressed in a U.S. Navy uniform.

- John F. Kennedy was the youngest man (43 years old) to be elected president. Ronald Reagan was the oldest (16 days short of age 70).

The President's Cabinet

The cabinet is made up of fifteen men and women who advise the president. He does not have to take their advice because there is no law that says the president must have a cabinet. Members are chosen for their experience and knowledge about a particular area of government. They meet with the president once a week in the Oval Office. The policies set by the president and his cabinet often result in new laws. Cabinet members serve at the pleasure of the president and can be fired at any time. Members include the following:

Secretary of State—recommends foreign policy

Secretary of the Treasury—recommends economic policy

Secretary of Defense—runs the Pentagon

Attorney General— is in charge of the Justice Department

Secretary of the Interior—protects our natural resources

Secretary of Agriculture—helps farmers and ranchers

Secretary of Commerce—supports the free-enterprise system

Secretary of Labor—protects the rights of laborers

Secretary of Health and Human Services—supervises federal medical programs and ensures safe food and drugs

Secretary of Housing and Urban Development—ensures that Americans have decent places to live

Secretary of Transportation—provides safe, affordable travel

Secretary of Energy—protects and regulates energy resources

Secretary of Education—responsible for all education

Secretary for Veterans' Affairs—provides veterans' benefits

Secretary of the Environment—protects environment and enforces pollution laws

The Branches of Government

Executive Branch

The President
Executive Office of the President
The Vice President

The Vice President

Legislative Branch

The Congress
Senate   House

Judicial Branch

The Supreme Court of the
United States

Answer Key

Page 5

1. natural-born citizen, 35 years or older, U. S. resident for 14 years
2. four years
3. If he commits a crime, he may be impeached by a $2/3$ vote of the House of Representatives.
4. commander in chief—directs movement of armed forces

   head of state—negotiates peace, trade policy, signs and vetos laws

   Ceremonial—award medals, greet visitors, light Christmas tree, laying a wreath on the Tomb of the Unknown Soldier

Page 32

1. food and rent were expensive, and inflation was high.
2. took their hard currency.
3. he set up smaller banks to handle government money.
4. they issued paper money of little or no value.
5. he wanted to set up a new U. S. Treasury.

Page 38

1. Amy Carter
2. William Wallace Lincoln
3. Chelsea Clinton
4. Elizabeth Tyler, Alice Roosevelt
5. eight, six
6. Scott Russell Hayes
7. Esther Cleveland

Page 44

Fact A
1. $330.56
2. $.73

Fact B
1. $812.50
2. $260,000,000.00

Fact C

Answers will vary depending on classroom size.

Page 74

1. High tariffs on imports caused the Treasury surplus.
2. Prices fell because the extra money was taken out of circulation.
3. President Arthur set up a commission to study reducing the tariffs.
4. Republicans wanted to continue the high tariffs. Democrats favored lowering the taxes.
5. The money could have been used to build roads, parks, or public buildings. People could have been given low-interest loans to buy homes or invest in their own businesses.

Page 92

What is a monopoly? It is when businesses combine to eliminate competition and control the market.

How might the merger benefit the companies? They lower their operating costs by eliminating duplication of jobs and equipment.

What might be the effect on the employees? Some might lose their jobs or be forced to relocate.

Explain why it is necessary for the government to control corporate mergers. It is to the advantage of consumers that there are competitive products in all markets. Competition creates job opportunities and keeps prices reasonable.

Page 113

1. It was unbelievable destructive power; it is awesome.
2. Secretary of War
3. He wanted to use the atomic bomb.
4. The Japanese ignored the warnings.
5. He believed it would save the lives of American soldiers.
6. Hiroshima and Nagasaki

Page 125

Problem – Five men were caught burglarizing Democratic headquarters.

Reporters – Bob Woodward and Carl Bernstein

Crimes – planting listening devices, covered up crime with hush money, stole confidential papers about Vietnam, tapped phone lines

Prosecutors – Archibald Cox and Leon Jaworski

Results for Nixon aides – convictions and prison sentences

Articles of Impeachment – obstruction of justice, abuse of power, and failure to comply with congressional subpoena

Result for Nixon – pardoned by President Ford

Bibliography and Resources

Black, Wallace and Jean Blashfield. *America Prepares for War*. Macmillan, 1991.

Blasingame, Wyatt. *The Look-It-Up Book of Presidents*. Random House, 1993.

Boorstin, Daniel J. *The Landmark History of the American People* (vols. 1 and 2). Random House, 1987.

Chant, Christopher. *Presidents of the United States*. Gallery, 1990.

Clark, Philip. *The American Revolution*. Marshall Cavendish, 1988.

Clark, Philip. *The Civil War*. Marshall Cavendish, 1988.

Dolan, Edward. *America in World War II*. Millbrook Press, 1993.

Encyclopedia of Presidents. Children's Press, 1987.

Fisher, Leomard Everett. *Stars and Stripes Our National Flag*. Holiday House, 1993.

Gordon, Patricia and Reed C. Snow. *Kids Learn America!* Williamson Pub. Co., 1992.

Greene, Carol. *Presidents*. Children's Press, 1984.

Hargrove, Jim. *The Story of Presidential Elections*. Children's Press, 1988.

Hills, Ken. *World War I*. Marshall Cavendish, 1988.

A Kid's Guide to Washington, D.C. Harcourt, Brace, Jovanovich, 1989.

Kennedy, John F. *Profiles in Courage*. Harper and Row, 1955.

Kent, Deborah. *The White House*. Children's Press, 1994.

McGowen, Tom. *World War I*. Watts, 1993.

McGowen, Tom. *World War II*. Watts, 1993.

O'Neill, Richard and Antonia D. Bryan. *Presidents of the United States*. Smithmark, 1992.

Parker, Nancy Winslow. *The President's Cabinet and How It Grew*. HarperCollins, 1991.

Phillips, Louis. *Ask Me Anything About the Presidents*. Avon Books, 1992.

Pimlott, John. *The First World War*. Watts, 1987.

Provensen, Alice. *The Buck Stops Here*. HarperCollins, 1990.

Ray, Delia. *A Nation Torn*. Lodestar, 1990.

Rubel, David. *The Scholastic Encyclopedia of Presidents and Their Times*. Scholastic, 1994.

Scriabine, Christine Brendel. *The Presidency*. Chelsea House, 1991.

St. George, Judith. *White House*. G.P. Putnam's Sons, 1990.

Sherrow, Victoria. *The Big Book of U.S. Presidents*. Templar, 1994.

Smith, Elizabeth S. *Five First Ladies*. Walker, 1986.

Stein, R. Conrad. *The Great Depression*. Children's Press, 1993.

Waricha, Jean. *George Washington Was Not the First President*. Parachute Press, 1992.

Teacher Resources

Degregorio, William A. *The Complete Book of U.S. Presidents*. Random House, 1993.

Kane, Joseph Nathan. *Facts About the Presidents*. H.W. Willson, 1993.

Sullivan, George. *Mr. President*. Dodd Mead, 1984.

Web Sites

The First Ladies of the United States of America
http://www.2.whitehouse.gov/WH/glimpse/firstladies/html/firstladies.html

Grolier Online's *The American Presidency* http://www.grolier.com/presidents/preshome.html

IPL Potus—*Presidents of the United States* http://www.ipl.org/ref/Potus

Welcome to the White House http://www.whitehouse.gov/wh/Welcome.html